God Works
Through Faith

Dr. Robert A.
Russell

Audio Enlightenment Press

Giving Voice to the Wisdom of the Ages

Printed in the United States of America

0 1 2 3 4 5 6 7 8 9

ISBN 978-1-941489-34-5

www.AudioEnlightenmentPress.com

www.MetaphysicalPocketBooks.Com

Audio book available on iTunes

God Works Through Faith

Dr. Robert A. Russell

TABLE OF CONTENTS

INTRODUCTION

This is the second in a series of books in which each title begins with the words, "God Works." I do not apologize for the repetition in the title or in the content. The human Mind tends to learn great truths, scientific principles, and mathematical facts slowly, or so my own experience leads me to believe.

Can you remember your struggle with addition combinations? How many repetitions did it take for you to master the multiplication tables? Parents are often impatient with the persistent questions of children about the facts of life which have been conscientiously presented to them, and sometimes attribute these to a morbid curiosity. It isn't that. It is merely an indication that the child has not been able to accept the explanation given "Him" and to make it his own in one experience.

No day goes by that doesn't teach me more about the way in which God works and more about what the power of Faith can accomplish. I learn from my own experience, from observing the lives of others, and from reading the words of persons who have deep convictions.

In this book, I have centered my discussion on Faith.

Dr. Robert A. Russell

CHAPTER 1

WHAT FAITH IS

Did you ever contemplate the things that happen through Faith—not the things that could happen, or the things that might happen, but the things that do happen, the things that are happening now?

Where Did Faith Come From?

You were born with the characteristic of Faith, for it is inherent in man.

Protected from the moment of your conception, you emerged into the world with the expectation of continued security.

You accepted the loving care of your parents—food, shelter, guidance—without question.

You not only accepted but demanded in a loud imperious voice the things that gave you emotional and physical comfort.

You took your first steps in confidence in the loving hand that held you, and you were not too discouraged by a few bumps and tumbles.

You smiled and expected a smile in return.

Today you walk to your work or drive or take a bus, expecting to arrive at your destination all in one piece.

You accept a job, expressing Faith in your potential.

You marry with Faith in the one you have chosen and Faith in your power to provide for your family.

In other words, you have Faith in yourself, and that is actually Faith in the God within you.

You eat food prepared by countless hands that you never see and wear clothing made by persons you will never know.

1

You trust the taxi driver to take you to your destination, the barber to shave your face, and the cook to prepare your meals.

How do you know that the taxi driver won't take you to some out-of-the-way place and hold you up?

Or that the barber will not cut your throat? Or that the cook will not poison your food?

Because of your Faith in your fellow-man and that too is Faith in the one God, who according to St. Paul, is above all, and through all, and in you all.

Three Gifts Are Yours.

When man walked out from God's finished thought, he bore three gifts:

Life: Energy, Animation - by which to live.

Mind: The power to reason, select, understand, and know, by which to become aware of God, of "Him"self and his environment.

Faith: Trust, confidence, assurance by which to penetrate the invisible and to hold God's promises until they are realized in "Him" and for "Him".

What Is Faith? The St. James version of the Bible says:

"Faith is the substance of things hoped for, the evidence of things not seen."

Moffatt translates the words in this way:

"Now Faith means that we are confident of what we hope for, convinced of what we do not see. What comforting words: evidence, assurance, conviction, substance"!

Faith is the belief that you have the power to do all things.

Faith is a magnetic power that attracts the answer to your prayer. Results do not come by chance, accident, or fate. They are molded by your Faith in your power through God.

Faith is the glass under the faucet; it is the water wheel under the fall; it is the windmill adjusted to the wind; it is the sunflower facing the sun; it is the ear at the telephone.

Success reduced to its lowest and simplest terms is Faith expressed in action.

Faith is a mental attitude against which there is no possibility of contradiction. If that attitude is directed toward God, it becomes your ability to do anything.

When you pray or treat, you have a right to expect an answer to that prayer or treatment, providing your conviction is in line with the nature of God.

Your Mind, however, must be so convinced of its idea, it must so completely accept it, that contradiction or denial is impossible.

When you have absolute Faith, there is nothing left in you to contradict your treatment.

Faith is the bridge between the physical and Spiritual world. You have the privilege of crossing on it at will

Faith not only makes old things new, but it is the point of contact between God and man.

Faith is the means by which we identify ourselves with the Allness of God.

Through our Faith, God fulfils His promises.

Through our Faith, His Good becomes visible and usable.

Desire is impressed upon the Subconscious Mind through feeling.

Chapter 1: What Faith Is

Faith holds the idea of desire in Substance until it takes form.

Faith is the most dynamic and transforming force in man.

To become mighty in the individual, Faith needs only a chance to exercise itself.

As students of Truth, we must work for the highest and most complete state of Faith, for Faith is the wire along which Omnipotence moves.

In that state, there is no longer anything in us to deny, doubt, or divide the Truth that we affirm.

We shall never perfect our Faith, however, by talking about it, reading about it, waiting for it or wishing for it; we perfect it by applying it to every phase of our living, to the little as well as to the big problems in our lives.

Faith is not just a stirring-up of the imagination.

Faith it is an actual power which acts upon our words.

Faith enables us to see things as God sees them, without blur or distortion.

Faith not only leads man into a definite course of action but opens the way for the Power to flow along the uncongested circuits of his thought.

No longer hampered by doubts, fears, and worries, man becomes, as Emerson says:

"The inlet and the outlet for all that there is in God."

The highest Faith is whole, continuous, triumphant, and victorious. It admits no contrary evidence, no fear, no opposition, no separation, and no limitation.

Hope says that it could happen or it might happen.

Faith says that it will happen.

4

Chapter 1: What Faith Is

Faith is the moving force in all creative processes.

Faith is the agent of healing, of prayer, and of demonstration.

Faith is the power to accomplish all things through Christ. All things are yours; and ye are Christ's; and Christ is God's.

The man of Faith experiences Wholeness.

"Thy Faith hath made thee whole", said Jesus to the woman who touched His garment in search of healing, to the blind beggar, Bartimaeus, and to the leper who returned to give glory to God.

Faith is an Individual Power.

Why did Jesus pinpoint thy Faith?

Why not the Faith of someone better trained or better equipped Spiritually than you recognize yourself to be?

He was showing us that the whole process takes place within the individual Consciousness, within my Consciousness if I am seeking the rewards of Faith, within yours if you wish to experience Wholeness.

Why do we ask for another's help? Why do we have practitioners?

When the evidence of the senses seems to overpower us, when we cannot see Reality through the cloud of false evidence, we are often impelled to seek the help of one whose vision is not obscured by our problem.

But unless we meet the Faith of the helper with one- hundred percent agreement, we are no better off than we were. Our Faith is still essential.

The Answer Precedes the Problem.

Do you remember the place in which Jesus could do no mighty works because of their unbelief?

Could healing not have taken place in Nazareth?

The Truth is that "the works" were already done Spiritually in that place as they are in all other places, but they had to await the recognition of the people concerned before they became visible on the material plane.

Do you see now why it is your Faith that makes you Whole?

Faith makes you Whole because in reality you are Whole already.

Your Faith simply acts to reveal that which already is. The works come automatically to the heart that believes.

We do not see the Law of Faith, but we know its power by what it does.

Our task is fourfold:

1. To become aware of that which eternally is The Omnipresence of God.

2. To claim the good we desire through Faith, Recognition, and Realization.

3. To accept the desire as fulfilled.

4. To realize our Oneness with God until the feeling of fulfillment comes to us.

Faith is the realization that ALL GOOD IS IN INSTANT MANIFESTATION.

If our prayers were not answered, if our needs were not met before we prayed, there would be no point in praying.

Jesus said:

"Before ye call I will answer and while ye are yet speaking I will hear. Whatever needs to be done is already done. Whatever is needed is already supplied."

There is no Life apart from God. There is no Power apart from God. There is no Substance apart from God. There is no Health apart from God.

There is no Being apart from God.

There is only ONE Mind, Life, Power, Substance, and Love in which we live and move and have our being.

When we get the realization of this Truth, the whole outer world changes.

Discordant factors are harmonized, problems are solved, difficult tasks are made easier, diseases are healed. The tenor of our lives becomes harmonious.

Faith Acts on the Level of Our Consciousness.

Life is a state of Consciousness.

Nothing can come to us except as Consciousness. Consciousness is all that we are, all that we are aware of, all that we believe.

We add to Consciousness or take from Consciousness with every experience.

The level of our Consciousness determines our Faith and that level of Faith is of our own making.

Faith is the starting point of every affirmation, prayer, and treatment; but without recognition of it as evidence of the Father Within without awareness of the closeness of our relationship to "Him", without acceptance of His promises, without the realization of the Omnipresence of God, it is likely to end as wishful thinking, daydreaming, or mere desire.

As you rise in Consciousness to the awareness of your Oneness with God, you will discover that there is no place for negation.

It is not person, place, or thing. Therefore, it has no reason for being.

Disease is a negative Faith operating through man, but it isn't the man and therefore does not belong to him. That is why you must separate the belief from the believer in your own Mind.

If evil had as much power as good, the universe could not exist for a second.

According to Jesus, you must empty the Mind before you can reach a heavenly state.

He that loseth his life shall find it.

When you lose your sense of personal power, the God Power awaits your use.

If God is, He is all there is, and all things are possible to you because of your Faith or conscious Oneness with "Him".

Now don't tell the world how wonderful it is until you have proved it for yourself.

Faith without works is dead.

The primary purpose of Spiritual therapy is not to make unhappy people happy, or sick people well, or poor people rich.

It is not to solve problems or to establish better and healthier living conditions. These are results.

The primary object is to help people realize the Presence of God.

To Become Acquainted with God. To Become Self-Empowered.

Eliphaz told Job in the midst of his suffering:

"Acquaint now thyself with "Him" [God] and be at peace; thereby good shall come unto thee."

To most Christians, God is a name rather than a warm and living Presence.

Christians talk about "Him", sing about "Him", read about "Him", preach about "Him", and pray to "Him"; but very few of us take the time or trouble to get acquainted with God.

How, then, can we know "Him" as a very present help in trouble?

When will we learn that Faith cannot lift us any higher or take us any further than the level of Consciousness on which we function?

That it cannot take out of Consciousness something which is not already there? Or that it cannot give us anything that is not already given?

If I want to know about electricity, how to use it and how to direct it, I associate myself with electricians who are experts with dynamos, motors, copper wires, switches and transformers; through them I come to the realization of electricity.

If I want to know about music, I associate myself with outstanding musicians, with musical instruments and compositions; through them I come to a realization of music.

If I want to know about painting and how to paint, I engage the best teacher I can find, I associate myself with artists, with paints, brushes, and canvas. I study the masterpieces of the world, and through all these, I come to a realization of painting.

If I want to get acquainted with you, I must identify myself with you. I must associate with you and be a companion to you. I must give you my thought and time. I must study your Mind and your nature.

If I am to understand you, I must know all about you. I must surrender to you.

How then does one get "acquainted" with God? How does one get to know "Him"?

Only by Practicing His Presence.

God must become to us a living, pulsating Presence.

God must become as real as our friends or the members of our family are to us.

We must know "Him", not as a cold and lifeless name, not as a vague and misty personality, but as an actual, living Partner.

The first function of Faith is to make God real—to make "Him" as real to us as He was to Jesus, John, and Paul.

Where is God?

Within each one of us.

Not within us in the sense that He is within our body, our solar plexus, or our brain, but within our Consciousness.

I and the Father are one.

When you realize that God is not in one place and you in another, when you understand your Oneness with "Him" and can say and believe I and the Father are one, your word will accomplish that whereunto it is sent, according to the promise.

When you believe that your desire is already fulfilled, believe that what you are asking for is already yours, you have put your Faith to work and what you seek will be manifested in your experience.

You have the word of Jesus that this is so, for He said:

What things soever ye desire, when ye pray, believe that ye receive them, and ye shall have them. . . . And all things whatsoever ye shall ask in prayer, believing, ye shall receive. . . . Before they call, I will answer; and while they are yet speaking, I will hear.

There is nothing on earth you cannot have. There is nothing you cannot heal.

There is nothing you cannot be if you have Faith enough to accept the fact that what you are seeking is already yours.

The fact that you can visualize a changed condition is proof of the Spiritual Reality of it.

By your Faith in the God with whom all things are possible, the desired condition materializes.

I can of mine own self do nothing. . . . The Father that dwelleth in me, he doeth the works. . . . He that believeth on me, the works that I do shall he do also. . . . All things are delivered unto me of my Father.

In this Oneness all things are yours. The ears of the deaf are unstopped. Blind eyes are opened.

Diseases are healed—not by using the Spiritual to heal the physical, not by using will power to force others to conform to your way of thinking, not by the application of brute force, but by the uncovering of the Perfection that is already there.

Too long have we had God in one place and man in another.

Too long have we kept apart that which God hath joined together.

Do you understand, you who are reading these lines? You do not have to acquire anything, buy anything, or create anything. You have only to accept your Oneness with "Him" through Faith.

Believest thou not that I am in the Father and the Father in me? . . I and my Father are one. . . . The Father that dwelleth in me, he doeth the works.

Could there be a stronger statement of Oneness, of Integration?

God is all Life. God is your Life. God is Mind.

God is your Mind. God is Power.

God is your Power.

Why is the Consciousness of Oneness so necessary to the perfect outworking of Faith?

Because it supplies the inner forces of Faith.

It acts as a magnet to draw to itself everything it needs for expression.

Solomon said:

With all thy getting, get understanding.

Without this inner force, the Consciousness of the Allness-of-God and our Oneness with "Him", Faith is partial, limited, and incomplete.

It becomes what some teachers refer to as "blind Faith" in contrast to understanding Faith.

Did you ever try to demonstrate over a problem while keeping your attention on the problem? What happened? You still had the problem but in a magnified form.

How Big Is Big?

Jesus' one and only formula for meeting trouble was Have Faith in God.

With Faith you can solve the apparently irreducible problems and remove the presumably insurmountable obstacles in your life.

You can dominate every circumstance. You can open every door.

It doesn't matter what the circumstance, condition, or problem may be.

If ye have Faith as a grain of mustard seed, ye shall say unto this mountain, Remove hence to yonder place; and it shall remove; and nothing shall be impossible to you.

Jesus likens human problems and troubles to mountains, but He says that if you have Faith, you can remove these mountains.

Faith can cause mountains to be swallowed up and lost sight of forever.

All your sickness and troubles can be reversed when you have a radical belief in God and an unqualified and unquestioning acceptance of the fulfilment of your desires.

But you must trust your Faith in the same way that the air-borne infantryman trusts the parachute that is bringing him to earth.

If ye have Faith as a grain of mustard seed . . . nothing shall be impossible to you.

Jesus did not say that fulfilment depends upon argument, reason, theology, logic, or a particular concept of God, but upon Faith.

Faith the size of a mustard seed is not a lot of Faith, but note the power Jesus assigned to it.

Of course, the mustard seed has an amazing potential for growth. So does the small Faith that you plant in the subjective Mind if you tend it carefully.

Perhaps the Faith you have now is just enough Faith to let you try Faith. Tend the seed with Love and confidence. Water it with persistency and tenacity. Shelter, the tiny growth from the cold winds of negative thought.

Visualize the effect in your life of Faith in action. See yourself using Faith.

See yourself living Faith.

See yourself expressing Faith.

Accept the promises made to those who believe as made to you personally.

Know that any desire you hold in Faith is a Reality in Spirit, existing from the moment you conceived it and eagerly awaiting its manifestation in your life.

Put your Faith to the test. Exercise it. Let it grow.

Why did Jesus use the mustard seed as a symbol of Faith?

To show the infinite power of even a little Faith.

The mustard seed is not only one of the smallest of seeds, but it is one of the most powerful and productive of creative things.

And so it is with the little bit of Faith.

With Jesus, the lesser Faith was always the promise of the greater Faith.

It doesn't matter how small your Faith is, if you believe in it, if you have Faith in it, if you keep it alive, if you keep it in motion, it has to grow.

Never allow yourself to minimize your "mustard seed" of Faith.

Never allow yourself to think of your Faith as inadequate.

Know that you have it and that you couldn't lose it if you wanted to. Praise it. Let it grow. It will do wonders for you; nothing shall be impossible to you.

Let us think of it in this way.

In the "mustard seed" stage, my Faith is like a little candle in the Mind. It gives forth a certain amount of light. But it is governed by impersonal law; it works the way I use it. If it works slowly for me at first, that is because my expectations and mental equivalents are small. I need to step them up. I know that a little steam will lift the lid of a tea kettle but a lot of steam will lift tons.

The Law of Faith is just that simple:

With what measure ye mete, it shall be measured to you again.

The manifestation of my Faith is not measured by the size of my Faith but by the acceptance, belief, or mental equivalent which I hold.

If I want a 500 candle power light, I must have a 500 watt globe. If I want the good measure, pressed down, and shaken together, and running over, I must present a large measure.

Thousands of people go every year to Shrines and Blessed Pools believing that they have some magic power to heal.

Hundreds who have Faith are healed through contact with these places.

But thousands return unhealed because they do not have the necessary Faith.

The Law of Faith.

According to your Faith—your Faith in God, your Faith in yourself, your Faith in your goal, your Faith in your ability, you get results.

The man of little Faith gets small results; the man of big Faith gets large results.

According to your Faith be it unto you.

That is just like saying that a gallon jug will hold only a gallon of water.

We can never go beyond the realization of our mental equivalents.

We shall never experience a good which is beyond our capacity to conceive and to receive.

This whole problem of belief and realization is just like using the muscles.

Today we can lift twenty pounds; tomorrow we can lift twenty-five. But there is no limitation to our capacity for Spiritual growth. We always express what we are. As much goodness as we can accept, that much we can demonstrate.

Sickness doesn't have to be, but until we know it doesn't have to be, it will be.

When we know that limitation doesn't have to be, there will be nothing to be limited.

All that I have is thine.

Are you a beggar sitting on a bag of gold?

Are you slumbering on the brink of the Infinite power?

Behold! You stand this day at the entrance to a land of tremendous possibilities.

Son, thou art ever with me, and all that I have is thine. This all is yours if you have the Faith to accept it, if you believe that you already have it, if you let it manifest AS YOU.

Seek ye the Lord while He may be found. Call ye upon "Him" while He is near. When is He near?

When you accept your Oneness with "Him", when you know that you have no Mind, Life, Substance, or Power apart from "Him".

What a light would come into our lives, what invincible power would come into our Minds, what a cleansing of the soul and body would result if we made use of this inner force of Faith!

New wine, Jesus called it—wine that bursts old wine skins of limited patterns and demands a new Consciousness to hold it.

We don't need new Faith or more Faith to be transformed.

We need only to renew our Faith in the Faith we already have.

Come, my friend. Make your contact with God through Faith.

The way of attainment is wonderfully simple and accurate.

It is not the way of the conscious Mind, of human thinking, or the way of teachers. It is the way of Spirit. I am that I am. I am the way.

In all thy ways acknowledge "Him". In all thy ways acknowledge His Presence, and It will guide you into all truth.

In "Him" we live and move and have our being.

Can God be any closer to us than our Consciousness of Omnipresent Good?

Can God be any closer than here?

Then rest from your anxious labours; release your tensions and your fears.

In the Consciousness of Oneness is your salvation.

When you pass from belief to realization, when you live and move and have your being in Omnipresent Good, Omnipresent Good lives and moves and has its being in You.

How much longer are you going to wait before you release this tremendous power within yourself?

Have Faith in God.

WAYS TO STRENGTHEN FAITH

1. Be expectant, confident, optimistic.

2. Keep your enthusiasm strong; never allow yourself to be discouraged or depressed.

3. Charge your Mind with interest, enthusiasm, ambition.

4. Keep your ambition and aspiration high; cultivate patience and perseverance.

5. Keep your imagination centred in what you want and keep your Faith moving toward it.

6. Keep your Consciousness expanding, growing and moving to higher levels.

7. Be positive in your thought, feeling, and action.

8. Accentuate the positive in every situation. Never allow yourself to dwell upon misery, sickness, operations, symptoms, reverses, misfortunes or bad luck.

9. Never depreciate, criticize, minimize or speak disparagingly of yourself. Never dwell upon your mistakes. Think always of yourself as growing, expanding and becoming more efficient, resourceful and dynamic.

10. Look for the good in everything and everybody. Refuse to recognize anything but the good.

11. Seek the best of everything and know that your Mind will produce it.

12. Think in large terms. The more you expect, the more your Faith will bring to you.

13. Convince your Mind that what you seek is already here, that it is yours now.

14. Train your Mind to think in terms of abundance; never allow it to dwell upon lack or limitation in any form.

15. Stimulate your faculties and talents by increasing your demands upon them.

16. When you meet trouble of any kind, refuse to be worried or disturbed by it. Know that you are bigger than any adverse thing that happens to you and have the power to overcome it.

17. Meet every problem with the conviction that it is already solved. See it as an opportunity to prove God.

18. Face every difficulty with courage, strength, and fortitude; determine to turn it to good account.

19. Know that you have the power to adjust anything, change anything, correct anything, overcome anything, or subdue anything.

20. Act always with the Truth; and never allow yourself to compromise with evil. If the Truth is to make you free, you must rely upon it. You must pass from belief to trust.

21. Believe the unbelievable. God goes all out for you when you go all out for God.

CHAPTER 2

HOW FAITH WORKS

Through Faith we understand that the worlds were formed by the word of God, so that things which are seen were not made of things which do appear.

The American Translation of the Bible clarifies these words:

It is Faith that enables us to see that the universe was created at the command of God, so that the world we see did not simply arise out of matter.

Moffatt translates the same passage in this way:

It is by Faith that we understand that the world was fashioned by the word of God, and the visible was made out of the invisible.

Before life becomes meaningful, before religion has any significance, you must face these questions:

1. Do you recognize man as more than physical, more than intellectual?

2. Are you also aware of the Spiritual man?

3. Do you recognize that there are Spiritual forces at work, in the world?

Your answer, of course, is yes or you would not be reading this book.

You would not be searching for a satisfactory explanation of God and of your relationship to "Him".

You would not be trying to find a pragmatic religion. You would have no desire to learn more about Spiritual Laws, no ambition to grasp the means of communication with Spirit which are available to you. You would not want to know how Faith works.

The persistence of man's recognition of his need for God and his unceasing search throughout the ages are proof in themselves of the Reality of the God he seeks.

What he calls God is not particularly important.

What he does with his belief is of supreme importance, for it determines the circumstances of his life, the conditions under which he lives.

Faith Works Through Acceptance.

A Unitarian minister, James Freeman Clark, once said:

"All the strength and force of man comes from his Faith in things unseen. He who believes is strong; he who doubts is weak. Strong convictions precede great actions. The man strongly possessed of an idea is the master of all who are uncertain or wavering. Clean, deep living convictions rule the world."

Someone has defined Faith as "the unconditional acceptance of the truth of our affirmations and an absolute belief that our desires will be fulfilled.

"Faith is not presumption but assumption. It is believing something which the conscious Mind says is not true.

Volumes could be written on the subject, but let us try to boil the process down into a few words:

To be successful in Faith we must not only assume (believe) that God is able, willing, and eager to help us, but we must also accept our responsibility to cooperate with "Him".

How do we cooperate?

By our realization and trust that He is fulfilling our every expectation NOW.

Our work is to make those facts real to our Minds.

I can speak the word of Peace, Health, or Prosperity, but unless my feeling supports the word that I speak, it accomplishes nothing.

It is only when my word and my feeling unite that I become One with the Power.

Why is this true?

Because feeling is the shock that sets the Divine Energy in motion.

There is a powerful Spiritual Law at work here. It doesn't make any difference what your problem or difficulty may be, if you will bring your Faith and your feeling to bear upon it, if you will realize that right now and always, there is an Infinite Power waiting to fulfil your slightest or greatest wish, you don't need to seek the solution. It will seek you.

The Law of Faith.

According to your Faith be it done unto you.

The Universal Response will always be in direct ratio to the degree of your expectation.

To "Him" that hath [the Consciousness of fulfilment shall be given. From "Him" that hath not [this Consciousness] shall be taken away even that which he hath.

If you expect much, you will receive much. If you expect little, you will receive little.

The Law Must Be Fulfilled.

The Law works equally well, however, when It is brought to bear on negative thought and feeling.

If you concentrate on ill-health, poverty, loneliness, injustice, and futility, these conditions manifest in your life according to your Faith.

The first thing to determine is the kind of Faith you have.

When you wish good to materialize, you must have a positive, constructive Faith. Then you are in a position to strengthen and develop it.

Perhaps your Faith is only the residue from the background of your childhood; maybe it is a little shrivelled from lack of use or tattered and worn from misuse.

You still have it, however.

All it needs is your awareness of its power, your recognition that you already have it in your possession and the opportunity to express itself in action.

Assume now that you have all the Faith in God that you need. Then act in accordance with this assumption.

Every affirmation, thought, feeling, word and action that expresses Faith impresses Faith upon the inner Mind. As the Subconscious accepts the impression, it will set in motion forces that are Faith-producing.

When we fill the Subconscious Mind with Faith— thoughts of Faith, feelings of Faith, memories of acts of Faith—by some mechanism of creation, we have Faith. The Law of Action and Reaction is at work.

The impression is an act of Faith; the reaction expresses the power of Faith.

The Subconscious Mind is the creative phase of Mind. The Subconscious Mind acts on what is given to it but does not originate anything.

But not every thought and feeling penetrates to the Subconscious fortunately.

We cannot always determine which of the many impressions we receive in the course of the day will go beyond the conscious Mind—the Mind of the senses—the top of the Mind.

Whatever passes through this Mind and finds lodging in the subjective Mind is quite likely to be pregnant with feeling of some kind.

But we have learned that we can deliberately plant in the Subconscious Mind the mental equivalent of the thing we should like to have objectified in our lives, that we can nullify thought that has been implanted for years, and that we can protect ourselves from the effect of a disastrous thought if we are aware of our danger at the time it threatens.

God Works Through Silence.

That is why it is a good idea to spend a certain amount of time each day impressing Faith upon the Subconscious.

We call this period the Silence.

When you are alone and relaxed, shut out the world, become very still and make your declaration of Faith.

Even though you have a hard time affirming Faith, affirm it anyway.

Even if you don't feel that you have it, say that you have it. Say, "I have Faith in God."

Say it positively and with feeling. Feel it down deep in your heart.

Know that every thought you think and every word you speak contains the mountain-moving power of Faith.

Concentrate on the meaning of the word Faith. Visualize the effect of Faith in action in your life.

See yourself moving in a world in which you meet men of Faith, men in whom you put your trust—a world in which you prove your own Faith by the authority with which you speak and act, by your calmness and poise and fortitude under difficulties, by your resiliency when stress has been removed—a world in which All things work together for good.

The promise reads:

"All things work together for good to them that Love God."

Paul told the Galatians that "nothing availeth anything . . . but Faith which worketh by Love. Thanks be to God."

We speak of enlarging our Faith, but the only way in which we can do this is by enlarging our mental equivalents, by increasing our demands and by adding the quality of gratitude.

When we believe that God wants through us the thing we want, we are ready to give thanks in advance.

George W. Wilson says:

"Possession follows the feeling that you do possess the things desired, and that feeling is made stronger if you will express gratitude for the possession."

"What things soever ye desire . . . believe that ye receive them, and ye shall have them."

When one is grateful for something he has not yet seen or touched or experienced as the result of his conviction that it already exists, his gratitude will hasten its arrival.

Have you ever noticed that praise of a dog brings out the best in him and that praise of a man inspires him to be and to do his best?

So it is with Faith.

Many delayed healings have come when the sick have applied the power of praise and thanksgiving.

The Conscious Mind Is an Agent.

There is a tendency on the part of some metaphysicians and schools of thought today to disregard the conscious Mind—to negate it or to ignore its activities.

This is, of course, foolish on the face of it.

The conscious Mind is not only the Mind of awareness and recognition, but the instrument that starts the Mind working in the chosen field of thought.

It senses and selects those ideas which it wishes to entertain.

Jesus said:

"Ye shall know the truth, and the truth shall make you free."

Without the activity of the conscious Mind, we cannot know or be aware of anything.

Acceptance of Truth begins in the conscious Mind as recognition or awareness; it is conveyed to the Subconscious Mind through realization or feeling.

We become aware of ideas. Through conscious thought we impress these ideas upon the Subconscious Mind.

This does not mean that we are going to use the conscious Mind to solve problems, heal disease, or to demonstrate prosperity.

We are going to use it for the purpose for which it was intended—an agent to help us become aware of the Omnipresent Good.

Science tells us that within the human body there are more than fifty million cells, each of which is a miniature universe and each of which lives its own life.

The Psalmist declares that Heaven and earth are full of thee, which means that GOD IS EVERYWHERE EQUALLY PRESENT.

God is Omnipresent.

God actually lives in each one of these cells at the same time.

Each one is a manifestation of God Consciousness.

If we live in the Consciousness, I and my Father are One, our bodies are vibrant with Life, Spirit and Health.

In the presence of Perfection, every cell expresses that Perfection.

We do not treat against arthritis, neuritis, appendicitis, tonsillitis, sinusitis, bursitis, colitis, nephritis, or any other specific physical difficulty.

In fact, the more we treat against a thing, the more we fasten it upon ourselves and the more real it becomes to us.

Why is this true?

Because a treatment against anything is virtually a treatment for that thing.

Disease is the effect of a cause implanted in the Subconscious Mind.

We overcome disease by realizing that the body is Spiritual Substance—an extension of Spirit in perfect form.

I and the Father are one.

The great purpose of Jesus' message was to teach us to realize our Oneness with God.

When Peter recognized and acknowledged the Christ in Jesus, the Master blessed him.

Lazarus is dead, said Jesus, but nevertheless He commanded, Lazarus, come forth. And so He commands today.

Throw off the grave clothes of your former self. Lift yourself a bit closer to the Allness-of-God. Why repeat the race history of Adam?

Why carry yesterday's ills, problems, and disappointments over into today?

Know ye not that the prayer of Faith shall save the sick?

Hath it not been revealed to you that the Son of man is come to save that which was lost?

Be still and know.

The most wonderful Statement of Being known to man is:

"I and my Father are one".

Meditate upon it and make it your own.

Take it into the stillness of your Consciousness and let God reveal "Him"self to you.

Be still and know that I am God.

Let His Life, Substance, and Power flow through you AS YOU.

Open your Mind to the truth of your Oneness with "Him".

Apply it to your body. Yet in my flesh shall I see God.

Make your contact with "Him" and say:

I KNOW THAT MY BODY IS SPIRITUAL SUBSTANCE.

NOTHING CAN FASTEN TO IT THAT COULD NOT FASTEN TO PURE SPIRIT.

SPIRIT COULD NOT BE SUBJECTED TO DESTRUCTIVE ACTION; THEREFORE, NOTHING DESTRUCTIVE CAN OPERATE IN ME.

THE INFINITE PERFECTION OF SPIRIT IS NOW WORKING IN EVERY CELL OF MY BODY, FOR I AM ONE WITH IT.

I ACCEPT MY HEALTH, MY WHOLENESS, WITH GRATITUDE.

Actually there are no healers of disease; there are only revealers of health.

Get rid of the festering, smouldering, soiled, smelly, disease-producing thoughts in the Mind.

Empty out all the mental waste that has been accumulating for years.

Flush out all the enmities, doubts, fears, jealousies, and worries by reversing them.

Claim your Oneness with God, and all these poison pockets will be drained.

You will understand for the first time the meaning of Jesus' words: Yet in my flesh shall I see God.

When Naaman the Syrian dipped in the Jordan seven times, his flesh became as pure as that of a little child.

So will ours when we know each new cell as perfect. Dr. Alexis Carrel of the Rockefeller Institute says in Man the Unknown:

"There is unquestionable proof of the efficiency of prayer in the cure of all diseases."

The documented story of the cure of tuberculosis, cancer, and other stubborn diseases by its use has been told many times.

Praying without ceasing is the constant recognition of our Oneness with God.

Healing emanates from a Consciousness of Wholeness.

Health is a state of Consciousness, a creative, upbuilding force that can turn weakness into strength, disease into ease, limitation into plenty.

It is this realization that makes prayer effective and practical.

When you get yourself out of the way of the divine circuits, the King of Glory will come in.

When you find God within yourself, the prayer will be answered.

"Prayer," says Kahlil Gibran in The Prophet, "is but the expansion of yourself into the living ether. When you pray, you rise to meet in the air those who are praying at that very hour, and whom save in prayer you may not meet. Therefore let your visit to the temple invisible be for naught save ecstasy and sweet communion. I cannot teach you to pray in words. God listens not to your words save when He "Him"self utters them through your lips."

Prayer is the realization of our Oneness with God and the acceptance of the tremendous power this realization gives us.

Someone has likened Faith to a bicycle.

"It stands upright only when it is in motion. The minute it stops moving, it flops on its side."

Faith must be kept in motion if it is to have power. It must be exercised to be of use.

Open mine eyes.

Have you found God?

Where are you seeking "Him"? God is Spirit, said Jesus.

But no one has ever seen Spirit.

If you say, "I will believe only what I see," you are living in darkness. You are in bondage to yourself, and you cannot know anything beyond yourself. You cannot know God. You cannot know Christ. You cannot know life. You cannot know Power. No one has ever seen God, Life, or Power.

If you believe only what you see, you must doubt your own existence. You have seen the house in which you live, but you have never seen yourself. What you see in the looking glass is but the form of your outer self. All you see of your Loved ones is the body house in which they live. The Real Self you have never seen.

If we accept the appearance for the fact, we are denying our true selves.

We exclaim with Job:

"Behold I go forward, but he is not there; and backward, but I cannot perceive "Him": On the left hand, where he doth work, but I cannot behold "Him": He hideth "Him"self on the right hand where I cannot see "Him".

Man is . . . full of trouble.

Are you easily discouraged?

Do difficulties pile up on you to such an extent that you tend to lose heart?

Then remind yourself of Jesus' words:

"In the world ye shall have tribulation [trouble]: but be of good cheer; I have overcome the world."

Settle this thing in your Mind once and for all. Did God promise a soft and easy life?

Did God promise that life here would be a bed of roses?

Did God say that there would be no crosses to bear, no problems to solve, no obstacles to climb over, no vicissitudes to meet?

God did not.

Then what is His plan for us? We have it in Jesus' own words:

Be not conformed to this world: but be ye transformed by the renewing of your Mind.

In other words, Be in the world but not of it. Go out and live life.

Fight the good fight of Faith. Keep the Faith.

Take unto you the whole armour of God [Consciousness of Truth] that ye may be able to withstand in the evil day, and having done all, to stand.

Of course you will have trouble in an unfinished world, but be of good cheer; I have overcome the world. [I have given you the Mind and Power with which to meet the world.]

It is true that you can skip a lot of trouble on the experience plane.

In fact, you can often transform trouble by letting this Mind be in you which was also in Christ Jesus.

You can ward off a lot of grief by practicing the Presence of God.

But trouble touches everyone at some time.

In the world ye shall have tribulation because it is that kind of world.

Then why be negative, pessimistic, and tragic about it?

Why single yourself out as a special target for trouble, saying as it hits you, "Everything happens to me"?

After all, we are not like the bewildered little boy who was lost in a Dry Goods Store. When a sympathetic floor walker stopped to ask what was wrong, he replied, "Please, Sir, have you seen a lady without a little boy who looks like me?"

We, sorely tried and troubled as we are at times, do have a Father and "closer is He than breathing and nearer than hands and feet."

In "Him" we live, move, and have our being. . . .

Being justified by Faith, we have peace with God through our Lord Jesus Christ. . . .

And not only so, but we glory in tribulations also. Perfect as this statement is, St. Paul went a step further. He went on to say:

"And we know that all things work together for good to them that Love God."

Do you see what the Apostle is trying to get over to us?

It is simply this:

No matter what befalls us, the secret of meeting it lies in bringing the power of God to bear upon it.

If we face trouble with the desire to learn from the experience, we shall rise victorious.

If it were not for trouble, there would be little mental or Spiritual growth.

Channing Pollock, the great playwright, once said:

"Men and motor cars go forward by a series of explosions. A beautiful motor car cannot fulfil its function until it has a series of internal explosions.

Just so a human being with conflicts and difficulties to overcome gets somewhere and becomes someone."

Make Your Agreement.

The first step in dealing with trouble is to agree with it.

Agree with thine adversary quickly whiles thou art in the way with "Him", says Jesus.

In other words, accept trouble as one of life's inevitables in the world Mind, see it as carborundum under the knife, realize that it can minister to the soul's higher good.

Crises, failures, hardships, pain, suffering, opposition, and injustice are nothing more than explosions in the mixing chamber of the Mind.

Agreement not only robs them of their power but takes the fear, fire, and sting out of them and conditions the Mind and life so that God can do greater things for us.

St. Paul said:

"Put on the whole armour of God."

If the explosions tear you apart, you have not made your agreement with trouble.

You will not be able to withstand in the evil day. St. Paul did not say:

"Put on part of the armour of God," but specified the whole armour of God. You must give "Him" your whole heart, Mind, soul, and strength.

"The Faith that saves," says John A. Redhead, "is the total response of the whole self to the will of God. It is the response of the Mind in belief, the heart in trust, the will in conduct."

I have known all kinds of people in all kinds of trouble, but it is only those who wear the whole armour of God who triumph over it.

Do you see why agreement is so important in meeting trouble?

It is one of the great factors in every successful demonstration. It determines whether trouble makes or breaks us, whether we go up or down.

The next step in meeting trouble is to cleanse the Mind.

Drop the trouble for the time being as you would drop a hot potato until it cools.

Get clear away from it in your thought. This may take time, but keep at it.

To receive the answer to any problem you must not only seek guidance, but must also present an open and untroubled Mind ready to receive it.

The solution cannot come while the Mind is running like a trip hammer.

Be still and know that I am God.

In quietness and in confidence shall be your strength. Get the Consciousness of His Presence.

See "Him" walking by your side.

Know that you are surrounded by a Creative Mind that receives the impress of your thought and acts upon it.

Know that you are in this Mind and that this Mind is in you.

Don't discuss your trouble with others and don't ask for advice; seek the answer within.

If the Subconscious state of your thought denies what your conscious thought says, it neutralizes the conscious thought.

That is why St. Paul told us to pray without ceasing. To get results you must pray until your conscious thought believes and the Subconscious thought no longer denies.

You must pray until all doubts are removed. Treatment is a mental and Spiritual adjustment; it is conditioning the Mind so that it no longer refutes the idea of Perfection embodied in the treatment.

It is important to seek God's guidance in every problem, but we must first make sure that we are actually and wholeheartedly putting our problem in God's hands.

Let us be childlike enough to believe that He will give us a definite and clear-cut answer.

It doesn't make any difference how difficult or how pressing the problem may be, it will ultimately disappear or be solved.

If you can be calm and collected in the midst of trouble, you will triumph over it.

If you can fill your Mind with the precious qualities of courage, confidence, and Faith, nothing can defeat you.

When the Subconscious Mind gets a new idea (when the idea takes possession of the conscious Mind), it gets you.

When you empty the Subconscious of all adverse, tense, troublesome, and distorted thoughts and fill it with thoughts of life, power, victory, and optimism, the whole tenor of your life will change.

"But this is such tedious work," you say.

That is right, but so is anything that is worthwhile and lasting.

Don't be misled by the printed or spoken word.

Many people say to me after listening to a lecture, "It sounds so easy when you tell us about it," and I know that is true.

Faith is easy to understand but hard to apply.

If it were otherwise, Christianity would soon lose its power.

Faith is a challenge.

If you are going to say the prayer of Faith, you must not only back it up with acceptance, belief and trust, but you must empty your Mind of everything that contradicts or denies the prayer.

That is why St. Paul said, our conversation is in heaven.

It is difficult to think and speak constructive, positive, happy, victorious, life-giving words when the Mind is filled with anxieties, apprehensions, antagonisms, antipathies, doubts, criticisms, and fears.

Just when some great challenge or opportunity comes along which would enrich our lives or improve our circumstances, we are stopped dead in our tracks by a sense of doubt, fear, or inferiority.

Some sinister thought wriggles up out of the Subconscious Mind and says, "Beware! This is not for you. You are not equal to it. You do not have what it takes. Let it alone."

Let not your heart be troubled.

Are you in some kind of difficulty right now?

Then start drawing upon your Faith. Face the difficulty and say:

GOD IN THE MIDST OF ME IS ABLE TO CONQER THIS THING.

HE IS DOING IT NOW.

I HAVE FAITH TO MOVE MOUNTAINS, AND I AM CALLING UPON THAT FAITH NOW.

I HAVE THE COURAGE TO CONQUER AND SUBDUE ANY ADVERSE THING.

But here comes that voice again, "You are only kidding yourself. You are scared stiff. You haven't any courage and you know it."

How are you going to silence this voice?

You are going to challenge it every time it speaks. You are going to make it tell the truth.

Say positively, forcefully, and with feeling:

SUBCONSCIOUS MIND OF ME, I AM TIRED OF YOUR LIES, AND I COMMAND YOU TO TELL THE TRUTH. I COMMAND YOU TO RESTORE MY COURAGE AND FAITH, AND I COMMAND YOU TO DO IT NOW.

Speak as one having authority.

Let the Subconscious know that you mean what you say.

Imagination Is a Gift.

Call upon your imagination. See yourself as you wish to be.

See yourself possessing the things you desire to possess.

Marcus Aurelius once said:

"A man's life is dyed by the colour of his imagination."

Imagination is the process of projecting images upon the screen of the Mind.

You don't have to go through a lot of mental gyrations and exercises.

You don't have to argue, reason, or divide.

You just make a picture—you become aware of something—you know something.

Raise the Level of Your Consciousness. Would you have God?

Then you must accept "Him".

You must become aware of "Him". You must be conscious of "Him". Do you see that?

Do you understand it?

Let me put it another way.

Can you have anything unless you are conscious of it? Can you eat a peach unless you are conscious of it? Can you drive your car unless you are conscious of it?

Can you greet a friend unless you are conscious of something?

What did Jesus mean when He said I am Alpha and Omega?

He meant that the whole Creative Process begins and ends in God.

There is nothing before Alpha, and there is nothing after Omega.

This is the whole operation; this is the way the Law works.

I AM A AND Z.

The A of Life is Consciousness, awareness; the Z is demonstration.

Put Imagination to Work.

Jesus gave us another wonderful concept.

Whatever you can imagine is yours, and you cannot demonstrate anything on the material plane that you cannot imagine first.

And all things, whatsoever ye shall ask, believing, ye shall receive.

Now ponder that statement for a few moments and make sure that you understand it.

Creative imagination is a Divine Faculty given to every man.

You have it now.

When you put it to work, it opens your Consciousness.

"But that is ridiculous," someone says: "Imagination is fantasy. It is a waste of time."

Do you know that you can't imagine anything that doesn't have a basis in fact?

Even your wildest and sometimes horrible imaginings result from putting together parts of things you have seen or read or heard about.

You say, "I want a better position," "I want a new house," "I want more friends," "I want to travel," "I want a larger income."

You know that each of these things has a factual basis. Then meet the test.

Answer the question: Can you imagine it?

Do you know that I and the Father are one? Do you know God AS YOU?

Do you have acceptance?

Do you have self-completeness?

If you have, what you want is yours.

You have taken it into Consciousness; it exists for you.

It objectifies as you. It is you.

If you can imagine it, you can have it.

If you cannot imagine it, you cannot have it. That is Principle.

"Whatsoever things you desire when you pray, believe that ye have received them and ye shall have them."

You say, "I want a farm of my own," "I want to be a great chemist (engineer, minister, leader, surgeon, etc.)"

Why not?

The desire is Spiritually legal—that is, it harms no one.

The wish is already established. That which you wish to be IS.

The Kingdom of Heaven is finished.

God's work is already done.

You are that which you wish yourself to be right now. Then why are you looking inside instead of out?

Why are you wishing instead of being?

Is it because you have something else mixed up in your picture?

Do you also say, "I am too old," "I am too poor," "I do not have enough education"?

But the power is right there. It is within you.

You could not have a desire that is not already established in God, one that is not awaiting your Faith to be objectified.

The farm is within you.

The engineer is within you. The minister is within you. The chemist is within you.

But you have to imagine it, believe it, feel it, embody it, dream it, become it.

The Everlasting Now.

There is no time in Spirit.

The fields are already white unto harvest.

The Kingdom of Heaven is at hand. But there must be immediacy in your prayer.

That promotion, that new refrigerator, that trip to Hawaii, that thing you are seeking to demonstrate—if imagination says "next year," Consciousness says "next year" and God says "next year." But Jesus says, "Thy kingdom come in earth as it is in heaven."

Note that IS.

Behold, now is the accepted time; behold, now is the day of salvation. The time of God's giving is always NOW.

Does anything happen when you pray? Does your word have power?

Is it backed by Faith and acceptance?

Do you accept your good with every cell in your body?

Do you feel it clear down to the tips of your toes?

What is the word that the metaphysician talks so much about? It is thought.

"In the beginning was the Word, and the Word was with God, and the Word was God. . . . And the Word was made—flesh".

Do you see what we are talking about?

This word you speak in the Consciousness that you are One with the Father is not a word of the head but a word of the heart.

It is the word of God. It is God.

Speak the word only and my servant shall be healed.

The word which is to be spoken into manifestation is a part of the whole. It is spoken with the understanding that I and the Father are one.

Tell me, then, about your word.

Do you take it into Consciousness?

Do you speak as one having authority?

Do you believe that the desire is fulfilled before you speak or do you only hope that it is?

When does the word become God?

When you can say, I and the Father are one.

If you will go back and study the above paragraph carefully you will see that what we been talking about is Consciousness.

In the beginning was Consciousness—and the Consciousness was with God—and the Consciousness was God—and the Consciousness became flesh.

The power of the word is in the Faith and Consciousness back of it. The words that I speak unto you, they are Spirit and they are life. . . . So shall my word be . . .; it shall not return unto me void, but it shall accomplish that which I please. The accomplishing word is not only the Spirit-filled word but the believing word.

It is both the substance of things hoped for and the evidence of things not seen.

If ye have Faith [awareness and acceptance] and doubt not . . . ye shall say unto this mountain, Be thou removed and be thou cast into the sea; it shall be done.

Note the words, ye shall say.

Who is it that is going to speak the word that will cast this mountain of trouble into the sea?

Why YOU, of course.

You are the one who will speak this mountain out of existence.

Ye shall say means you who are reading this book. You Determine the Level of Your Consciousness. Look at your Consciousness for a moment.

What do you find there?

Which side of the fence are you on? What are you seeing?

What are you feeling?

What are you thinking? What are you accepting? Something evil? Something partial? Something poor? Something sick? Something feeble?

Well, whatever it is, that is what you will get and what you will continue to get until you want something else.

Just what are you seeking?

What is it that you are trying to do? What is it that you want to be?

Is it necessary for your fulfilment?

Will it add to your peace? Can you imagine it?

Look again and tell me:

Is it complete and finished in your thought?

Then speak your word and take the thing you seek. Don't muff it by fears and challenges.

Don't strain. Don't doubt.

Don't throw obstacles in the way. Just take it by Faith.

If thou can'st believe, all things are possible to him that believeth.

This is not the head belief of mental assent but the heart belief of Faith and trust.

Are you seeking that state of Mind by which the things desired become the things possessed?

Then you must come by the way of Jesus' appointing.

Seek ye first the kingdom of God [the Consciousness of ALLNESS].

Recognize your Oneness with it.

Unite your Mind with His Mind. Claim your Good. There is an old fable about a dog that boasted of his ability as a runner. One day he gave chase to a rabbit but failed to catch it. The other dogs ridiculed him on account of his previous boasting.

His reply was: "You must remember that the rabbit was running for his life; I was only after my dinner."

The incentive is all important. You now have the incentive.

If you are seeking loaves and fishes, you will not put the same quality of Consciousness into your search that you will if your ambition is deeper and more serious.

Seeking the Spirit back of things not only puts you in possession of things but enables you to use them freely.

It is the one thing that cannot be lost, stolen, fluctuate, or fail.

Emerson said:

"What a man does, that he has. What has he to do with hope or fear? In himself is his might. Let him regard no good as solid but that which is in his nature and which must grow out of him as long as he exists. The goods of fortune may come and go like summer leaves; let him scatter them on every wind as the momentary signs of his productiveness."

Knock, and it shall be opened unto you. Are your knuckles raw from knocking? Are your eyes tired from seeking?

Are your vocal chords parched from asking?

You set out to demonstrate health. You observe all the laws. You pray and treat. But nothing happens.

Perhaps you knock at the door for supply. Your need is desperate. The mortgage is due, and the creditors are breathing down your neck. But no one opens the door. What are you going to do? Pin crape on your sleeve and bemoan your fate? Are you going to become cynical, frustrated and embittered? Are you going to settle back in your defeat, shrug your shoulders and say, "What's the use?" Are you going to run up the flag of surrender and say bitterly, "It doesn't work for me," or more bitterly, "It doesn't work"?

The thing to do is to recognize that closed doors come to all alike.

It doesn't make any difference how good you are or how much you know, sooner or later you will come to doors that do not open.

You will resist them or you will use them, according to your attitude toward them.

If you see them as dead ends, you will go down under the belief.

If you ask, "Why?" and find the cause to be your own divided Mind, your lack of realization, you can make the necessary change within yourself and knock again. If you see them as tests of your Faith, you will continue to knock.

Did Peter become panicky, fearful, or hysterical when the door did not open?

Did he fly into a rage?

What do the Scriptures say? Peter continued knocking. What a lesson in that for us!

Our Faith is tested by our ability, having done all to stand.

It is tested by our ability to keep knocking.

Closed doors are often simply a series of questions concerning our fortitude and our stability; they are the measure of our Faith.

Can you be patient in the face of delay?

Can you be positive in the face of negation? Can you be dauntless in the face of defeat? Can you be confident in the face of ruin?

Can you be peaceful in the midst of confusion?

Can you maintain your Faith in the midst of doubt and uncertainty?

There is always the possibility that what you most desire is not the thing that you should have.

Can you not look back in your life and see occasions when the thing that happened was far better than the thing you projected?

A locked door may be side by side with one that is opened wide.

If you have a close relationship to God, it should be easy for you to trust everything in your life to "Him".

It should be as easy to give "Him" your problems, difficulties, and needs as it is to trust "Him" to develop the seeds which you plant in the ground or to regulate your heartbeats and the other involuntary processes of your body.

Of myself I can do nothing, but with God all things are possible.

All is All-there-Is.

You are a point of expressions for this Allness; but until you identify yourself with it, you are like an electric light globe with the switch turned off.

Why is the Consciousness of Oneness so important in Spiritual demonstration?

Because One with God is a majority, Walter Lanyon says:

"When you become one with anything, you become that thing, so to speak; so to become one with law is actually to become that law in action."

Now ask yourself:

"Am I the law of health in action? Am I the law of success in action? Am I the law of prosperity in action?"

If your answer is No, ask yourself, "Why not?" The answer you will probably get is this: "You are trying to contact God from a point outside yourself."

It is not by mouthing affirmations or singing hymns that God becomes a very present help in trouble; it is only by working from the Centre out, only by becoming the Law in action.

What must one do after he has impressed his desire on the Subconscious Mind?

He must trust God for the perfect outworking of the Law.

What does God ask of us? Just one thing—Faith.

Why do we complicate the process?

Is it wholly because we cannot believe that results will come from simply trusting?

Isn't our real trouble that we cannot quite let go? What does it mean to let go?

It means to close the bulkhead doors so tightly that they cannot be opened, to put our claim in an air-tight compartment that we no longer have access to, to go all the way in trusting "Him", and not to go back to the problem in thought until it is solved.

Is there anything so hard about that?

Not any more so than dropping a piece of paper in the waste basket and leaving it there.

You let go of your needs and wants, your ambitions and aspirations, your fears and your worries, your obligations and your responsibilities, your claims and your desires in perfect trust and abandonment, knowing that GOD TAKES HOLD WHEN YOU LET GO.

If you take them up in thought again after placing them lovingly in His hands, you only delay His action. You must trust them to "Him" with the same abandon that you drop a seed into the ground.

Jesus said that the seed must rot before the new shoot can come forth. It cannot rot, however, if you keep digging it up.

Do you see how stupid it is to try to force God to do your bidding and how wise it is to let "Him" express "Him"self through you AS YOU?

Do you want the peace and rest that come through Spiritual relaxation?

Then take your place in the Consciousness of Christ. Identify yourself with the isness of your Divine Self.

Clothe yourself in Faith, trust, assurance, receptivity, and gratitude and then beat upon the gates of Heaven with all the indomitability, importunity, persistence, and Spiritual strength which you have.

The secret of successful achievement is to press your claim persistently and consistently.

Do you understand the difference between instantaneous healing and gradual healing?

It is the difference between absolute acceptance and partial acceptance.

Instantaneous healing comes when you are able to accommodate the idea with which you have become One.

A thing is true because IT IS TRUE. You do not have to make it so.

"Blind Faith," someone has said, "follows God's Laws ignorantly and haphazardly and with intermittent results. Understanding Faith works with God's Laws harmoniously and successfully."

Prayer made in understanding Faith exerts a powerful influence.

When you have absolute Faith, it will be as easy to heal a cancer as a headache.

Do you believe that you are going to get the things you have asked for?

Do you feel it in every atom of your being? Do you realize it in your Mind?

Believe that ye receive them and ye shall have them.

In other words, accept your fulfilled desire in your whole Consciousness, nothing doubting.

"Assume a Virtue, If You Have It Not." Dramatize your affirmation, if need be.

Pretend to yourself that the desired condition is already established.

Live, think, act, and speak as though it were fulfilled now. If all things are possible to "Him" that believeth, the belief must come first.

Even though you are terrified by the thing that has happened to you, you must keep your mental level high.

Put on the whole armour of God.

Call upon your dynamic and creative Faith. Apply it to your problem.

Tell God that your Faith in His Power is limitless and that you are calling upon that Power now.

Realize that the Subconscious receives your directions and acts upon them immediately.

If God be for us [for me], who can be against us [against me]?

Repeat this statement many times.

Get your Consciousness of Oneness and partnership with God, and nothing can defeat you.

With every demonstration you make, your Faith will be nourished, vitalized, and strengthened.

You will come eventually to the place at which you will make your demonstrations easily and naturally.

You will build up within your Consciousness a magnetic field which will attract all the elements and factors needed for your success.

Why do you sit still?

There are factors that delay healing and other answers to prayer.

Through your objective Mind, you can identify these, reason about them and analyse yourself to see which of them are operating in your life.

By putting your Faith to work through your knowledge of how to use your subjective Mind (which is one with the Creative Mind of God), you can eliminate them.

Doubt not.

Doubt is one of the malignant forces that attempt to operate against Faith.

If ye have Faith and doubt not . . . whatsoever things ye shall ask in prayer, believing, ye shall receive. . . . Whosoever . . . shall not doubt in his heart, but shall believe that those things which he saith shall come to pass; he shall have whatsoever he saith.

We open the Mind through Faith and close it through doubt.

A kingdom divided against itself shall fall.

The ancient plea, *Lord, I believe; help thou mine unbelief* is made by each one of us at some time, for the objective Mind registering the impressions of the senses challenges *the substance of things hoped for, the evidence of things not seen.*

A very ardent young Lover began his letter to his fiancé in this way: "Darling, I'd swim rivers and seas to be near you. I'd climb all the mountain ranges in the world to be at your side."

But after pages and pages of sentiment he added this postscript: "I'll see you Sunday night if it doesn't rain."

So it is with us.

We say, "I would do anything to get more Faith," "I'd give my right arm to learn how to pray." But there is always the postscript, "I'll take up the study in earnest if I can find the time," "I'll take the course if it doesn't cost too much." *If* it doesn't rain, *if* it doesn't inconvenience me, *if* I can spare the money. The *if* betrays the divided Mind. St. James said, *A double- Minded man is unstable in all his ways.*

Dean Inge once said:

"We are losing our Christianity not because anyone is taking it from us, but because it is a religion for heroes, and we are merely harmless, good natured, little people who want to have a good time."

What does the Law say?

He that loseth his life shall find it. . . . And ye shall serve the Lord your God, and he shall bless thy bread and water; and I will take sickness away from the midst of thee. . . . Seek ye first the kingdom of God and his righteousness and all these things shall be added unto you. . . . Trust in the Lord and do good . . . and verily thou shalt be fed.

Only by continual discipline and practice can we become single-Minded, one-pointed. Our watch word must be *Emmanuel . . . God with us.*

"Think of self, trouble grows; Think of God, trouble goes."

Your Father knoweth that ye have need of all these things.

Outlining the process by which the aid we seek will come is another factor in delay.

We say, In thee is my trust, and then we tell "Him" how to do His work.

Are you still outlining when you pray?

Are you still trying to figure out when and how the prayer will be answered?

Turn on your trust.

Let go some more and keep letting-go until the problem is completely out of your hands.

The when is not important; there is no time in Heaven but now.

All you need to do is to follow the rules:

1. Ask.

2. If there is no answer, Seek.

3. If you still get no answer, Knock.

Put all the possibilities, probabilities, chances and likelihood's out of your Mind and give God a free hand to help you in His way.

Outlining is trying to get God to go your way.

My thoughts are not your thoughts, neither are my ways your ways.

For as the heavens are higher than the earth, so are my ways and my thoughts higher than yours. . . . Eye hath not seen, nor ear heard, neither have entered into the heart of man, the things which God hath prepared for them that Love "Him".

Be sure you understand the principle involved.

Let us assume that you are in need of financial help and that you are starting out to demonstrate supply metaphysically.

How do you go about it?

The first thing you do is to make your claim by impressing it with deep feeling upon the Subconscious Mind.

You assume the attitude that would be yours if the desire had already materialized.

You declare your Oneness with God's Allness, and you take the words of Jesus personally, Son, thou art ever with me and all that I have is thine.

You believe this promise and you accept it for yourself. Your Mind is now open to the things of God, and you are ready to take the final steps. There are three of them:

1. You call upon your creative imagination to help you see in your Mind the thing you want.

2. You feel God's power entering your treatment and accomplishing what you have asked for.

3. You claim fulfilment of your desire by saying, "In the name of the Father, and of the Son, and of the Holy Ghost. Amen."

Finally, you rest the case with "Him" in perfect trust. You know that if God cannot do it, it cannot be done.

The word Amen, which means so it is or so he it, is your recognition of the fact that God has already done everything that needs to be done, that you are already that which you want to be, that you already have that which you seek.

Are you ready to take the final step, or are you still wondering how your need for more money will be met?

Perhaps several possibilities run through your Mind: "Frank owes me money. Maybe he will pay me." "It's a long time since I had a raise. I could ask for one tomorrow." "Possibly someone will buy those lots." "Perhaps someone will leave me some money."

"Maybe it isn't God's will that I should have this demonstration."

The Law says that God can't take hold until you let go. Put all these possibilities out of your Mind and think only of God's power and His willingness to use it in your behalf.

He has ways of fulfilling your desires which you have not even thought of.

Cling to that trust.

Increase your understanding of it. Be true to it.

Dare to leave everything quietly to God.

Dare to claim His overflowing abundance in the midst of poverty and lack.

Dare to trust "Him" through every difficulty and every vicissitude.

Dare to claim that God can do, that God will do, that God is doing whatever is necessary right now.

Dare to acknowledge the Presence and Power of God in every person, circumstance, condition, and thing.

Know God in yourself AS YOU.

Do you feel the thrill and upsurge of power that comes to you as you say these words—God in Me AS ME?

It is I, be not afraid.

Fear, which is Faith in negative, is an agent of doubt and often the cause of it.

It is Faith misdirected. It is Faith in evil.

God didn't plant failure, limitation, trouble, worry, fear and disease in you. You thought them up yourself, fed them with your thought and attention, kept them alive with your belief and so continued to attract them to your experience.

How, then, do you expect "Him" to answer your prayers?

How can He get through a Mind choked with negation?

You cannot claim the blessing until you make room for it, until you identify yourself with it.

The Mind can think only one thought at a time; the sooner you give up your negations the better.

The Law is infallible, immutable, and inexorable. There is no evading It.

It works for you only as you bring yourself into obedience to It.

To receive directly from God, you must let go of everything unlike "Him".

Only then does all that the Father hath become yours. Here is a middle-aged man who is in a desperate situation financially.

He asks for Spiritual help and then explains all the reasons why he cannot get ahead.

"The cards are stacked against me," he says. "I have tried to find a job but no one wants a man over fifty. There are no opportunities for a man my age. There is no work in the town where I live and I have no money to go elsewhere. What good would it do anyway because the list of unemployed is growing everywhere? I am really not well enough to take a job if it were offered to me."

This sounds like an exaggeration but such a case is common. This man tells his practitioner that he is looking to God for supply and then enumerates all the reasons why He cannot succeed in giving it to "Him".

Why is such a man sick and poverty-stricken? Because he is misdirecting his Faith.

He is directing it into negative channels instead of positive channels. He is looking to God and looking away from "Him" at the same time. He does not know that it takes the same power to go forward as it does to go backward. Will his prayers be answered? Yes, in terms of more lack. Why? Because he is giving more power to his circumstances than he is to God.

How can he change the action of the Law?

How can he cause It to work for "Him" instead of against "Him"?

He can do it by changing his relationship to It.

This man reminds us of the disciples when the listening multitude needed to be fed. They were overwhelmed by the problem. Can't you hear them?

"We have here," they said, "but five loaves and two small fishes."

"My goodness! Is that all we have?"

"Are you sure? Don't we have anything else?" "That is all there is."

"Just five loaves and two measly fish! And five thousand hungry persons!"

"Let's tell Jesus to send them to the village to buy food. Of course, this is a desert place and it's already getting dark. But let's all go together and tell him what we think. We must save our faces."

Now listen to Jesus:

They need not depart: give ye them to eat.

You remember the end of the story. He blessed, and brake, and gave the loaves to his disciples, and the disciples to the multitude. And they all did eat and were filled: and they took up of the fragments that remained twelve baskets full.

You and I often face the five-loaf-and two-fish problem. We too tend to overstate our poverty and thereby increase it. We, like the disciples, forget how close we are to the Source of Supply, how near He is who came that we might have life and have it more abundantly.

It is one thing to affirm the Allness-of-God and another thing to make a connection with it. All that the Father hath is mine only when I am in His Consciousness, only when I have the conviction that it is already mine.

Jesus knew that the Law of Faith works negatively as well as positively.

When a man says, "There are no opportunities for one my age. Nobody wants a man over fifty. The cards are stacked against me. I never get the breaks. I am not well enough to take a job," and he believes, that . . . which he saith [accepts it as true], shall come to pass. What he believes will continue to manifest in his affairs. God is not unkind or unfriendly, but He works through Law.

Life responds to us by corresponding to our states of thought. It gives to us according to our expectations. The Law is impersonal. It works the way we use It.

Ye have not received the Spirit of bondage again to fear.

Bondage to the past that continues to be an active force in our thought and feeling and action can be escaped from only by accepting the promise.

Ye shall know the truth, and the truth shall make you free.

The subjective Mind is the seat of the memory.

Buried deep in it are the causes of much of the delay we experience in appropriating our good.

These unseen and forgotten forces tend to keep us in a state of restlessness and frustration.

To all outward appearances there may be nothing in your life that is contrary to the Law of God.

But you are troubled much of the time, uncertain, vague, jumpy and haunted by fears you cannot even name.

Do I hear you say that this does not apply to you? Then you are an exception to the rule.

Either that, or you have not honestly faced your delays, disappointments and defeats.

Have you ever desired something which despite all your best efforts has eluded you?

Have you ever entered one of those hectic periods when everything goes wrong and nothing goes right?

Most of us have suffered frustrations and disappointments and some of us have dwelt upon them until they have taken root.

Are you asking such questions as these:

What is this imperious voice which speaks out of the shadows and says no when it should say yes?

Why is my healing so long delayed? Why do my goals elude me?

Why this mental and Spiritual conflict within me?

How long must I continue half-slave and half-free? Do you really want to know?

Do you really mean to do something about it?

Then listen to Jesus:

"Ye cannot serve God and mammon."

You cannot follow two lines of thought and get one result.

You will continue half-slave and half-free until you cleanse the Mind and flush out every old fixed unhappy thought that enslaves you.

You may not recall when you first entered this unhappy state, but there is One in you that knows.

There is One who has provided a way out.

There is One who can make you wholly free, One who says, Come unto me all ye who are weary and heavy laden and I will give you rest.

Suppressed desires, forced inhibitions, race beliefs in such things as heredity and predestination, forgotten experiences that left remorse, resentment, hatred, jealousy, envy in their wake often prove to be the unknown forces that play upon our lives and express themselves in our experience.

Sometimes they are consciously accepted but most often they lie deeply buried in the Subconscious Mind but not dead. Accepted, they make wonderful alibis for shortcomings.

Have you ever heard anyone say such things as these?

"That's the way I was brought up. I can't change now."

"My father was tubercular and so I have never been strong."

"Of course, I'm afraid of lightning. When I was a child, mother used to send me under the bed."

"I forgave her, but I didn't forget and I just can't stand her."

"Oh, we'll always be poor. We always have been."

If you have any doubt about the effect of these fixed and unhappy thoughts that afflict most of humanity, observe their patterns in the lives of individuals.

Observe the effect upon the eyes, the face, the skin, the pulse, the manner of speaking, acting and thinking.

Anything in the Subconscious Mind that lowers the mental level lowers the vitality and drags down the health.

Dr. Frank J. Sladen of the Ford Hospital in Detroit, Michigan says:

"I maintain that a man cannot live without Christ unless he admits that living in unhappiness and conflict, in hate, envy, selfishness, futility, nervousness and fatigue, in slavery to innumerable possibilities of compensatory and destructive habits is really living.

"In my eyes, people come figuratively limping into church, handicapped and sick from living with unsolved problems within their own bodies, or their homes, or with their children, business or other relationships. Even if they don't realize it and don't consider themselves ill, they do resemble—going to and from church—our patients as they go to and from the office; except that the former wear their best Sunday clothes."

Many people try to demonstrate Truth while still filled with untruth.

It doesn't work.

Many people have accepted Christ in the conscious Mind but not in the Subconscious and here much of our conversion falls down.

When the dentist pulls an offending tooth, he knows that he must get the root or it will set up an infection that will poison the whole system later on.

So it is with these habit patterns of the past. Until the roots are withdrawn, the manifestation of Faith will be delayed.

These habit patterns that cause us to limp through life may have started as some little sin, fear, mistake or imagined hurt. As they were repeated, they gradually cut a pattern in the Subconscious Mind and all our thoughts from then on flowed through this pattern. Some of them got roots through repetition and others through repression or suppression.

We dwelt on them so long that they sank into the Subconscious and there formed a centre of their own from which, without our consent, they exert a constant power.

To a greater or less degree, we all have these unconscious influences in our lives, and fight them as we may, as long as the roots are there, our thought is drained through them.

There is a way to root out all these habit patterns of the past but it cannot be effective until the cause of the trouble is known. By that I mean that we cannot apply a constructive course of action until the offending pattern has been unmasked.

The first step, therefore, is to find this hidden memory pattern and to bring it out into the light.

Where does your trouble come from? When did it start?

What caused you to be so fearful? When did you first get angry?

Who was it that hurt you and why? Why were you resentful?

Why were you disillusioned?

What did you do that caused you to be ashamed? Why do you feel guilty?

Try to recall.

Get very still and try to remember.

Command the Subconscious Mind to bring all these memories up to the conscious Mind.

Do it in the same way that you recall a name, date or event.

Make your demand and then turn your thought to something else.

Whatever information you are seeking will come forth.

Does not the Bible say that:

"There is nothing covered that shall not be revealed; and hid, that shall not be known"?

The answer may come while you are in the Silence or it may come while you are thinking about something else, but come it will.

In the moment ye think not, the Son of man cometh. The next step is to replace the offending pattern that you have uncovered with one that is so strongly positive that it literally reverses the negative one.

Let us suppose that the offending thought pattern is fear—fear of any one of the thousands of things that hold people in bondage.

To reverse fear, enter the Silence and meditate upon a statement of truth such as this:

MY FAITH IN GOD DELIVERS ME FROM ALL FEAR.

Impress these words upon the Subconscious Mind with deep feeling until a great sense of peace (which is the answer) comes over you.

Then speak to your Subconscious Mind in some such manner as this:

SUBCONSCIOUS MIND OF ME, YOU ARE A VIBRANT LIVING PART OF ME.

YOU ARE INSTANTLY RECEPTIVE AND RESPONSIVE TO MY CALL.

YOU ALWAYS OBEY MY COMMANDS AND DIRECTIONS.

YOU FULFILL MY DESIRES TO THE LETTER. YOU ALWAYS DO WHAT I WANT DONE. THERE IS NOTHING THAT YOU CANNOT DO.

I HAVE ABSOLUTE FAITH IN YOU BECAUSE YOU ALWAYS ACT UPON THOSE IDEAS WHICH I FEEL TO BE TRUE.

YOU ARE ALWAYS WAITING FOR MY CALL, AND RIGHT NOW I WANT YOU TO REVERSE THIS PATTERN OF FEAR WITH A PATTERN OF FAITH.

ELIMINATE FROM MY MIND ALL FEAR AND ALL BELIEF THAT ANYTHING IS NOW WRONG OR EVER CAN BE WRONG.

INSULATE MY MIND AGAINST FEAR SO THAT NO THOUGHT OF FEAR CAN EVER ENTER MY CONSCIOUSNESS AGAIN.

YOU CAN DRAW THE ROOTS OF THIS OLD FEAR OUT OF ME AND I KNOW THAT YOU ARE DOING IT NOW.

GO ALL THE WAY BACK TO MY MEMORIES AND HEAL ALL THESE THINGS THAT HAPPENED IN THE PAST SO THAT THEY WILL NOT TROUBLE ME ANYMORE.

YOU HAVE RECEIVED MY INSTRUCTIONS AND YOU HAVE RESPONDED TO MY CALL.

YOU HAVE BROKEN THE CHAINS WHICH HAVE BOUND ME.

I FEEL THE FULLNESS OF PERFECT FAITH IN EVERY ATOM OF MY BEING.

MY FAITH IN YOUR POWER IS UNLIMITED AND I KNOW THAT THE HEALING FREEING WORK BEGUN IN ME WILL CONTINUE UNTIL I AM EVERY WHIT WHOLE.

Such a meditation may be used for any intention simply by changing the words to correspond to the nature of your desire.

Judge Troward said:

"Whatever we believe, does, for us, in very fact exist." That is true about these unconscious forces which, unchallenged, plague the Mind and life.

If you have a root pattern of fear, if you believe that the cause of your fear is real, it will be real to you. It will injure you quite as much as though it were real.

Therefore, change your Consciousness from the negative pattern into the positive pattern.

You must come to see that these doubts that darken your vision, these fears that paralyse your efforts, these ghosts that haunt you, these memories of people who represent opposition are really nothing more nor less than your own reactions to the things that have happened to you.

They have power only because you give it to them. Withdraw the power by reversing the pattern, and they will cease to trouble you.

When you have cleansed your Mind and brought it around to a normal, natural state, you will be able to say with Jesus:

"The prince of this world cometh and findeth nothing in me [nothing for evil to act with]."

When the stream of Consciousness is no longer diluted with doubts, fears, inhibitions, and repressions, Faith has an open channel through which to flow.

Energies will be quickened, resolution strengthened, confidence deepened, life broadened and enriched, and courage made sublime.

Several years ago, a prominent woman called to ask if I would come and pray with her for healing. She had a broken hip that would not heal, and I soon found in talking with her that the delayed healing was not in the hip itself. The doctor who had been called to set the hip after the accident had made a mistake and another doctor had to be called six months later to set the hip properly. X-ray pictures showed that the hip was then set perfectly but still it did not heal.

In questioning the woman further, I found that her heart was filled with bitterness and hatred toward the doctor who had made the mistake.

Her body was now filled with great pain and suffering.

"I must have relief," she said. "I believe that God can heal me."

"He can heal you," I replied, "if you give up this hatred, but He can't heal you so long as you are generating this poison in your Mind."

"Well, there is nothing I can do about that," she answered, "for I shall hate that doctor as long as I live."

"Very well," I replied. "Then there is nothing I can do for you."

Several months elapsed and the woman called again. This time I found her in a very different frame of Mind. "I have been thinking," she said, "about what you told me the last time you were here and I have decided to try to Love Dr. . . I want you to pray for me that I may be forgiven for the hatred I have been holding toward him."

God had touched this woman's heart and she saw for the first time that her Faith in God's power could not operate in the presence of her resentment, that Love and hatred could not dwell in the same place at the same time, and that without Love there would be no healing.

There was now a deep desire in her heart to be liberated from the feeling of bitterness and hatred which had been filling her body with pain.

She was ready for Christ to come in and break the chains of torment which she had bound around herself.

She was freed and her body was healed. Take Three Steps: Turn, Deny, Realize.

I like The Treatment Book written by F. L. Rawson many years ago. In it, he says:

"Turn in thought at once to Heaven." Turning one's thought is the first step.

He was saying practically what Jesus said:

"Thy kingdom come. Thy will be done, in earth [here, now, in you, in John, in Mary] as it is [being done] in heaven."

Any disease there? NO!

Any sudden death there? No death at all.

Any cancer there? No!

Having gotten the realization of the Heaven within you, pray for yourself or another, knowing that His will is that we be perfect here and now even as He is perfect.

Rawson said secondly:

"Deny the existence in Heaven of the wrong thing thought of, seen, or felt."

You are praying for someone with cancer.

Do you see what a boon it is to be able to say:

"There is no such thing in heaven. Heaven is within me and I am within heaven"?

And then to say, "Oh, God, Thy will be done, in earth [here in me, or here in my friend] as it is in heaven"?

"Thirdly," Rawson urges, "realize the existence of the opposite."

When we hold with sufficient tenacity to the Truth, that is, to the Reality of the Spiritual Plane, we get grace from above to change conditions on the physical plane.

The most powerful treatment you can get is the realization of the truth in the statement: I and the Father are One.

There is nothing more powerful than the Consciousness of Oneness with God.

As I write to you today, it is snowing. There is no argument about it. When you picked up this book to study, there wasn't anything in you that doubted it was a book. When you can say to a person with cancer, "You haven't any cancer," with the same conviction and realization that you say, "This is a book," there will be no cancer.

Man made the devil to oppose God, sickness to oppose health, poverty to oppose prosperity, hell to oppose Heaven, by his ignorance or his refusal to recognize and realize his Oneness with God.

But no matter how long he has been in the desert of duality, no matter how he has messed things up, the moment he accepts his Oneness with the Father, he becomes a new creature.

The thing he is seeking is the thing he will get when he believes that he has it.

69

The signs follow them that believe. Because God is, you are.

The very fact that you exist is proof that you are some part of the Whole, and on this rests your Faith.

You know THAT YOU ARE. Are what?

SPIRIT.

When the Prodigal Son in his destitution said, I will arise and go unto my father, he went unto his own Consciousness—the Presence of the Whole.

He said in substance:

"I shall arise from these human limitations and regain my Consciousness of Oneness with the Father."

Through Faith, you come to see that God is that Something within you that knows Itself.

The Lord thy God in the midst of thee is mighty.

When you demonstrate the Allness-of-God, you recognize that It cannot know anything other than Itself.

It includes everything. It is everything.

It cannot know anything separated from Itself.

As you turn to God, He turns toward you. I shall arise and go unto my father.

Father of what?

The Father of my body: the Father of my business; the Father of my work; the Father of everything in my world.

Like the Prodigal Son, you effect this union for yourself.

The Consciousness of the Presence is that state of Mind which believes in the good, the enduring, and the true.

70

When you dare to arise and go to the Father's house, you arrive by the way of your Oneness with God.

There is nothing in your Mind to contradict this Oneness.

You believe that your word is using a Power greater than Itself and that there is nothing in the Universe to deny it.

You accept the invitation, Call upon me, knowing that every demand you make upon the Presence will be honoured.

The Presence has only one purpose and that is to experience Itself in and through you.

You have only one purpose and that is to accept the Presence.

When you return to the Father's House, you change from self-Consciousness to God-Consciousness.

Why tarriest thou?

Arise: are you afraid to try your Faith? Are you afraid that it won't work?

Then dismiss such a foolish thought from your Mind.

Even while you are afraid that your Faith won't work, it is working.

It takes just as much Faith to believe that Faith doesn't work as to know that it does.

"What doth it profit, my brethren, if a man say he hath Faith, but hath not works?"

Can Faith save him? . . . By works a man is justified and not by Faith only. . . . For as the body without the Spirit is dead, so Faith without works is dead also.

Are you still trying to force your good into manifestation by concentration, through breathing exercises, through formulas or other gimmicks?

Be still and know that I am God.

If you would avoid the tiresome treadmill of making demonstrations month after month, lose yourself in the One. Leave all and follow me.

Speak the word only and my servant shall be healed. Thou shalt also decree a thing and it shall be established unto thee.

There stands the Truth towering like the Rock of Gibraltar above all your futile efforts!

God in the midst of you! God AS YOU!

Life AS YOU! Power AS YOU! Health AS YOU! Prosperity AS YOU! Do you say:

"If I had just had this teaching in my youth! If I could only have had it sooner!" Sooner than what?

Don't you know that when the student is ready the teacher appears?

The teacher is here. You are ready now. It is time to act.

Do something.

Put the Law to work. Take your stand.

Hold to it through thick or thin.

God works not by doing but by Being. He waits to express "Him"self AS YOU. Think of yourself as God in objective action. Think of "Him" in you AS YOU.

Know ye not that ye are the temple of the living God? Do you wish you had more Faith?

Are you waiting for it to develop before you make use of what you have?

To increase the potential of Faith, you must increase your expectations.

You must as Jesus said, Launch out into the deep. To become skilful in Faith, you must practice Faith.

Imagination shows you the possibilities of God's Kingdom; Faith makes them real.

Now is the accepted time.—Are you ready to put your Faith to the test?

Then get a pencil and paper and go to work. Put your prayer or treatment in words.

See the problem, not as your imagination reports it but as it is in Truth.

The answer awaits your application of the Law of Faith to bring it into manifestation.

The orderly outworking of the Law follows as naturally as day follows night.

Apply the rule and the answer follows. What is the rule?

Seek ye first the Kingdom of God and His righteousness and all these things shall be added unto you.

In other words, put first things first.

Seek first your conscious Oneness with God. I and the Father are one.

State as briefly as possible your intention—what you are seeking from God.

Be very accurate and definite.

Your formula (desire) must be just as clear and exact in your Mind as if it were projected on a moving picture screen.

73

Take these steps:

1. Release the desire with deep feeling to the Subconscious Mind.

2. Let God have it.

3. Don't question or wonder how the desire is going to be fulfilled. Dismiss any mental reservations or doubts.

4. Keep a positive image before your Mind.

5. Accept the outcome of your prayer.

A claim upon Truth is an affirmation, and affirmations like rubber balls have a way of bouncing back.

If results seem slow at first, take the intention into the Silence several times a day, impressing it with deep feeling upon the Subconscious Mind until you realize that the problem is already solved.

Then loose it and let it go.

Remember that A man can receive nothing, except it be given "Him" from heaven—from the Within.

When you establish the Consciousness of the Allness- of-God and your Faith in "Him" is absolute, the words, I and the Father are one, will become so meaningful, so significant to you that there will be no doubt, no delay, no fear, no buried-but-not-dead malignant thought to repress or inhibit the freedom promised to you.

Ye shall know the truth and the truth shall make you free.

Freedom from worry and anxiety releases your power to serve, develops appreciation of the beauty and magnitude of the world you live in, increases your joy in life.

Faith in God enables you to recognize that you are One with the Creative Principle which seeks constant expression through you.

You realize that your responsibility is to release It through your acceptance as a channel through which the Father's business is carried on.

Freedom from the fears and anxieties commonly associated with the body comes from knowing there could be no physical manifestation of any kind if there were no Spiritual Cause.

Happily relating yourself to others becomes a matter of recognizing the perfect Spiritual Man in each individual you meet and in accepting your common Oneness of purpose.

Faith enables your first waking thought to be This is the day which the Lord hath made; we will rejoice and be glad in it.

Are you ready to speak your word? Then close your eyes.

Relax yourself into God's Presence body, Mind, and Spirit.

Now hold the great desire of your heart in the forefront of Consciousness for a moment.

See it clearly. Get your sense of Oneness with God. Say with deep feeling:

"THIS IS GOD WANTING WHAT I WANT THROUGH ME."

QUESTIONS AND ANSWERS ABOUT FAITH

1. WHAT IS THE NATURE OF FAITH?

The nature of Faith is to act; it acts not because we make it act but because it is its nature to act.

Faith is the governing factor in our activities.

When Faith is directed toward anything or anybody, it acts of its own volition.

Faith draws to us that toward which our Faith is directed.

2. WHAT IS THE OVERALL MEANING OF THE WORD FAITH?

The general meaning of the word Faith is a positive Faith in God, the Good.

Faith is a mental attitude which places God at the centre of one's thoughts, words and acts.

Faith means an absolute trust in and reliance upon God.

Faith based upon Principle works when everything else fails.

3. WHAT IS MEANT BY A LIVING FAITH?

A living Faith is one that never doubts, falters or wavers.

Faith clings to Divine Law until victory is realized.

Faith not only believes but also accepts the fulfilment of every promise.

4. WHY IS FAITH CALLED THE KEY TO THE STOREHOUSE?

Faith is the causal factor in prayer.

Faith accepts the unreasonable and believes the impossible.

Someone has said, "Faith counts the things that are as though they were not, and the things that are not as though they were."

5. WHAT IS THE BEST TRANSLATION OF PAUL'S DEFINITION OF FAITH?

Moffatt's translation is the best rendering of this passage:

Now Faith means we are confident of what we hope for, convinced of what we do not see.

6. WHAT IS REQUIRED FOR AN IRRESTIBLE FAITH?

A consuming interest and a fixed desire are essential. The first is the driving power of Faith; the second is the adhesive force which holds it to its goal.

But desire and interest without Faith are helpless.

7. IS FAITH INTELLECTUAL OR SPIRITUAL?

Faith is essentially Spiritual.

Faith begins in the Mind but comes to fruition in the heart.

Faith is not measured by our intellectual ability to call a thing done, but by the realization in the heart that it is done.

8. WHAT IS THE DIFFERENCE BETWEEN FAITH AND BELIEF?

Belief is of the intellect while Faith is of the heart. Many people believe that they are one and the same thing, but that is not true.

There is belief in Faith, to be sure.

But, as the Bible tells us, the devils also believe.

Almost anyone can believe, but not everyone can exercise Faith.

Without the power of Faith, belief is weak.

9. WHAT IS THE DIFFERENCE BETWEEN BLIND FAITH AND UNDERSTANDING FAITH?

Blind Faith is an undeveloped Faith.

It follows God's laws ignorantly and haphazardly. Jesus spoke of the blind leading the blind.

Understanding Faith is a developed Faith which works with God's laws harmoniously and successfully.

10. WHAT IS THE DIFFERENCE BETWEEN HOPE AND FAITH?

The best answer to this question is contained in an old, unaccredited quotation:

"Hope is a draft on futurity, sometimes honoured but generally extended."

What does this tell you?

Why is hope a draft on the future? Why is it generally extended?

Because the future is a time apart from experience. Hope is honoured only when it becomes Faith.

The difference is that between possibility and actuality.

Hope is vague, uncertain, and sometimes forlorn while Faith is definite, certain, and joyous.

There is no delay in the answer to our prayers other than lack of Faith.

11. IS IT NECESSARY TO HAVE FAITH IN YOURSELF?

By all means, for Faith in yourself, in your Real Self, is also Faith in God.

It is the starting point in every worthwhile accomplishment.

If you do not have Faith in Yourself, how can you have Faith in God and in others?

If you do not have Faith in your ability, how can you put it to work?

To be successful in any field of endeavour, you must not only have Faith in God, but in Yourself and in others.

According to your Self-confidence, be it done unto you.

Believe you can and you will.

If you follow and trust God's laws, you cannot fail. Know Yourself, believe in Yourself, think well of Yourself.

Get rid of the worm-of-the-dust attitude.

Self-confidence keeps the Mind working at full speed and capacity and draws continuously upon the deeper resources within.

12. WHAT IS MEANT BY NEGATIVE FAITH?

Fear is negative Faith.

Before we can fear anything, we must first have Faith in it. In fact, there can be no fear without Faith.

Fear is Faith in evil.

13. WHAT IS MOST IMPORTANT IN FAITH?

The most important thing in Faith is its polarity.

If your Faith is positive, your thoughts will be positive, your words will be positive, and you will attract the best of everything.

If your Faith is negative, your thoughts will be negative, your words will be negative and you will attract the worst of everything.

The polarity of your Faith determines the results.

If you have been living, thinking, acting, speaking on the negative side of life, the polarity of your Faith needs changing.

14. WHAT IS MEANT BY THE WORDS, POLARITY OF FAITH?

This is explained fully in Making The Contact, but I shall explain it briefly here.

Faith is an attitude of the whole Mind but fulfillment depends upon how deeply it is embedded in the Subconscious.

Out of the heart [Subconscious Mind] are the issues of life, said Jesus.

No matter how much we may know intellectually, or how fervently we may pray, we always attract those things which we really are.

The Law of Faith works both ways.

If it is centered in the desirable, we attract the desirable.

If it is centered in the undesirable, we attract the undesirable. That is the Law of Polarity.

15. HOW DOES ONE REVERSE NEGATIVE POLARITY?

If Faith is moving in the wrong direction, moving with a negative Faith in evil, the only thing that needs to be done is to replace it with Faith in good.

Dr. C. O. Southard says:

"Faith is not subject to argument or experiment".

A person either believes or disbelieves; and since that Faith is fixed in his Subconscious, it can only be altered by the person "Him"self, by his own efforts."

Through the conscious Mind, we analyze the character of our Faith and make our decision.

By using our will, we give attention to that which is good.

What we give attention to becomes a moving force in our lives.

Our Faith in good expands and grows with use.

16. WHAT PART DOES THE SUBCONSCIOUS MIND PLAY IN CHANGING THE POLARITY OF FAITH?

The Subconscious Mind is the agent in changing the polarity of Faith.

First, you break up the negative habits of thought into which the Subconscious has drifted by cleansing, by discipline, and by reversal.

Then you condition it to hold the positive idea so firmly that it becomes the ruling factor in your thoughts, acts, and words.

This can be done in meditation and in the Silence by impressing the idea with deep feeling upon the Subconscious Mind, not spasmodically but consistently.

You can accelerate the process by repeating the idea to yourself silently or aloud even as you go about your daily tasks:

"My Faith is in God, Omnipotent Good, as the only Presence and the only Power in me and in my affairs."

As you do this, the old habit of thought will drop away and the new concept will take its place.

17. WHY IS DESIRE NECESSARY TO THE PERFECT OUTWORKING OF FAITH?

Desire is the matrix or mould through which Faith works.

It is the pattern through which demonstrations are made. Since the Law of Faith is impersonal and works for the bad as well as the good, and since we are continually believing in something, Faith must have a guide.

Whatsoever things ye desire when ye pray, believe that ye have received them and ye shall have them.

When the desire is drawn out to a point (clearly defined), it becomes a demand. Our claim must be specific. We must have a vivid mental picture of what we want and here the imaginative faculty comes in.

If you can imagine it, you can have it.

18. WHY MUST THE DESIRE BE FREED BEFORE IT CAN BE FULFILLED?

You might as well ask why the seed must be dropped into the ground before it can bring the increase.

Seed cannot grow in your hand, on the shelf, or in the packet.

Nor can your desire materialize if you hold it tightly in your thought.

Jesus told us to Take no thought in order to give the desire a chance to go forth and bring back its reward.

Since the desire cannot be in two places at the same time, we must choose between fulfillment or frustration, between letting-go or holding-on.

Jesus says that the seed must be dropped in the ground and that the desire must be relinquished to God.

Take no thought does not mean lapsing into a state of unconsciousness; it means taking away the anxiety and fear which prevent the manifestation of your desire.

When you release the desire in absolute forgetfulness, as Jesus did, the reward will come flowing into you in limitless measure. The way of fulfillment is not through thought but through God.

19. WHY IS IMAGINATION IMPORTANT IN SPIRITUAL WORK?

Imagination stimulates the faculties of the Mind.

It expands Consciousness and causes the Mind to act along new lines.

In metaphysics, we call it the great magnifier.

If you are seeking to demonstrate a new home, you first decide what kind of a home you want. You see it so clearly in Mind and in such detail that it is ever in the forefront of Consciousness. Then you proceed to desire that home with all the passion and power of your soul.

The next step is to imagine yourself living in that home, moving from room to room with the members of your family and looking after it. This is the pattern of your desire and you keep that pattern before your attention. You make it so complete and perfect that there will never be any occasion to change it.

Imagination calls forth the great or the small according to the directions which you give it.

Therefore, you must always seek the best, or that which is in accord with your highest ideals. You should never make provision in your thought for a compromise. If you have an ideal house in Mind, stick to that ideal. Apply all the power of your desire in making your dream come true.

20. WHAT PART DOES EXPECTATION PLAY IN FAITH?

Expectation is Faith in action.

Expectation is the feeling of fulfillment that comes from conviction.

When you ask God for something, you must Expect to receive what you ask.

Expectation that comes from conviction does not run around beating the air in anxiety and suspense like the bettor at the race track.

Expectation is calm, tranquil and confident. Knowing that the desire is already fulfilled, it is quiet, serene and undisturbed.

The Expectation that gets phenomenal results wastes no time in speculation or doubt but accepts the promises of God as real and true.

The greater your Expectation, the harder your Faith will work and the more it will accomplish. Expect the best, and you will get the best. Expect your Faith to work, and it will work.

Expectation is not only a great stimulus to action but is also the push and motive power behind Faith.

It causes your Faith to move with greater rapidity and power toward the fulfillment of your desire.

Have you decided what you want?

Then charge your Mind with tremendous Faith, interest and expectation.

Know that your Faith will produce it. Let your feeling of expectation be full, deep, and continuous.

21. WHAT PART DOES CONCENTRATION PLAY IN FAITH?

It is a mental law that any idea held firmly in the Mind expresses itself in the body and affairs.

But the only ideas that can be held firmly in the Mind are those in which we have Faith.

The purpose of concentration in Faith is to direct all our thoughts, feelings, and activities toward the fulfillment of our desire; in other words, to pinpoint the desire until it has been realized.

22. WHY IS PERSISTENCY NECESSARY TO SUCCESS?

Persistency in Faith is like fire under the boiler.

Faith generates the Energy necessary to success.

There is nothing that cannot be accomplished through Faith.

But the trouble with most persons is that they do not hold to their Faith long enough to realize the fulfillment of their desire.

They are up today and down tomorrow. Their Faith works by fits and starts.

They lack the stick-to-itiveness which brings success.

St. James says of such a person:

"He that wavereth is like a wave of the sea, driven with the wind and tossed. Let not that man think that he shall receive anything of the Lord." The Law says that if we want success we must have Faith and persistency. The promise is that In due season we shall reap if we faint not.

The faint heart cripples Faith and limits its capacity for worthwhile achievement. You cannot lose if you hang on.

23. WHAT PART DOES THE WILL PLAY IN DESIRE?

The will plays no part in desire. In fact, its only purpose is to determine whether you will believe or not.

Until the desire has been placed in God's hands and forgotten in absolute trust, you delay the manifestation which it is His purpose to bring to pass.

We do not will things into being.

We will only to initiate action and to start things going.

We will to act, to go forward, to achieve, to do more, and to be more.

We can achieve only what we will to achieve. We can do only what we will to do.

Will does not control Faith or mental action, but it does give impetus and push to it.

24. WHY IS IT THAT MANY PERSONS DO NOT REALIZE THEIR IDEALS?

They have not learned to will to believe; they have not learned to think what they want to think. Instead of acting from their own Spiritual centres, they act on the beliefs and suggestions of others. They follow borrowed ideas instead of their own, and their paths are strewn with incomplete and unfinished tasks.

The way to overcome this tendency to drift and wander is to stay put.

When you have made up your Mind, when you know that your desire is right and Spiritually legal, do not allow anything to influence you or cause you to change your Mind.

25. WHAT HAPPENS TO FAITH THAT IS NOT USED?

The same thing that happens to the tires on an automobile that is not used.

To keep the rubber flexible and resilient, the car must be used.

So it is with Faith.

Faith if not used, it becomes static and weak.

It is like a pool of water that is not agitated; it lacks power.

Just as our muscles develop through exercise, Faith grows through use.

The Law says, "Use or lose."

26. IS IT TRUE THAT NEGATIVE THOUGHT ACTS WITH GREATER POWER AND RAPIDITY THAN POSITIVE THOUGHT?

No, it is not; it only seems that way.

The force of any thought whether negative or positive is always in direct ratio to our Faith.

If we have more Faith in evil than in good, the results will be more negative than positive.

27. WHAT ARE THE SIX STEPS IN DEMONSTRATION?

The first step is to formulate our desire—to see it clearly in Mind.

The second step is to impress it with deep feeling upon the Subconscious Mind, to see ourselves accomplishing that thing.

The third step is to exercise our Faith by accepting the desire as fulfilled.

The fourth step is to keep our feeling and thinking moving with our desire.

The fifth step is to order our conversation aright—to speak always in terms of expectancy and fulfillment.

The sixth step is to carry our desire into action—to act as if it were already fulfilled.

CHAPTER 3

WHAT FAITH DOES

What does Faith do?

And now we are talking about Faith in God, not just a vague and unidentified feeling that there must be somewhere, somehow, a power that is greater than ourselves.

There are countless records in print of the effect of Faith in God; you can, no doubt, find instances in your own experience.

Have you never in a moment of crisis—a skidding car on an icy road, an apparently unavoidable collision with an approaching car, a desperate family situation involving illness, need, or tangled human relationships—called involuntarily on God for help and received it?

Here are three dramatic incidents drawn from my own records. I could devote an entire book to records of this kind, for they are endless. I have purposely confined the stories to extreme cases in which undeviating Faith served as the channel through which God moved.

Case I

Some time ago, a woman seventy years old fell down a long flight of stone steps and was rushed to the hospital. For four days she lay in a coma with a fractured skull and other serious injuries.

After three specialists in consultation had said the case was hopeless, I was called to the hospital in the middle of the night by a member of the family.

"The doctors have given her up," said the night nurse as I entered the room.

"Given her up!" I exclaimed. "What do you mean?" "There is no hope for her. She will probably die in the night," she explained.

"Aren't doctors the sworn enemies of death? What right have they to give up a woman who is still alive?" I demanded.

There was a strong vibration of despair and resignation all through the room; and as I sat by the patient's bedside, I asked the nurse if she would Mind leaving the room while I prayed.

"Not at all," she said graciously and quietly stepped out into the hall.

This was a crisis. I knew that I had to furnish God with transparency of thought and a clear, open channel to work through.

A radical Faith was needed at a time like this, and it was up to me to provide it.

A great sense of peace filled me as I entered the Silence and began to treat for the speedy recovery of the patient.

There was no response at first. Then, reaching through the rail on the side of the bed and taking the woman's hand in mine, I said:

"God, we are not going to let this woman die. She is needed in her great work and we want her to live. I am asking you right now to touch this broken and bruised body and to restore her to perfect health and wholeness. We believe that you are releasing the healing power of Christ in her this instant and that it is now penetrating and dispelling every negative and inharmonious condition."

Did she live? Of course she lived. Before the prayer was finished she regained Consciousness.

She turned to me, saying - "Why, Dr. Russell, what are you doing here at this time of night?" It was truly a resurrection.

On the second day after my visit, her chauffeur took her for a drive in her car. The third day she was taken back to her home.

Case II

In one of my healing missions on the Pacific Coast, there was a woman in attendance who had cataracts in both eyes. They had failed to dissolve through her own Spiritual efforts and prayers, but she insisted that her healing would come in the healing service always held the last night of the Mission.

Several of her devoted friends came to see me before the Mission started and asked if I would remember her in my daily devotions and instructions, promising that their Faith would be joined with hers and mine.

This woman was much Loved not only for what she had done for the community and the church but also for her beautiful Christian character.

I talked with her and explained the Prayer of Faith and how to fulfil the conditions for her healing.

She cooperated to the letter.

Day by day I could see the Creative Power coming to life in her. First, there was just a little stir; then there was a movement; and the night of the public healing service, the manifestation of the Presence was complete.

When she knelt at the altar rail and I laid my hands upon her head, I felt as though all the power of God were flowing through my hands into her eyes. I visioned this Power dissolving the cataracts completely and entirely and as I pronounced the word of healing:

"In the name of the Father and of the Son and of the Holy Spirit, I command these cataracts to be dissolved."

It happened.

There was a mighty rush of Spiritual Energy, the Energy of God working through our Faith.

By morning the cataracts were gone, and her vision was perfectly clear.

Why did I say "In the name of the Father and of the Son and of the Holy Spirit"?

Why didn't I say "In the name of the Father" or "In the name of the Son"?

Because there are three channels through which the Power comes.

1. There is the Father—that which is understood.

2. There is the Son which is understanding.

3. There is the Holy Spirit which is the expressing.

In metaphysical science, we refer to these as:

1. Awareness.

2. Realization.

3. Revelation.

The two healings described as well as the one that follows were all accomplished by the direct action of the Holy Spirit.

Some healers and preachers pray for the Holy Spirit as though He were a portion of something.

They think of "Him" as being in a far away place, but the chief field of His activity is in our own Subconscious Minds.

There are others who speak of the Holy Spirit as something to be used; they refer to "Him" as an "It".

When will we learn that He is a Presence and Power that uses us?

St. Paul tells us that if the Spirit of "Him" that raised up Jesus from the dead dwell in you, he . . . shall also quicken your mortal bodies by his Spirit that dwelleth in you.

We cannot use the Holy Spirit; He uses us. Why should we go in search for "Him" when He is already here?

He is wherever our Mind and Spirit make the contact with "Him".

The Holy Spirit, as the Nicene Creed tells us "The Lord and Giver of Life." He is divine replenishment to those who are ready and willing to be used by "Him".

He is power to rise triumphantly over every obstacle, to meet every need, to supply every lack and to heal every disease.

Listen to His promise:

I will pour out my Spirit upon all flesh. Are the organs of your body sluggish?

The Holy Spirit will establish perfect right action and harmony in them.

Is your circulation poor?

The Holy Spirit will cause the blood to circulate more freely.

Are your nerves shattered?

The Holy Spirit will steady them.

Case III

Being blessed with a mother of great Faith and Spiritual power and having seen many miraculous answers to her prayers, it is only natural that I should have grown up believing that Faith can accomplish anything.

Mother not only prays but accepts the answer to her prayer.

More than that, her Mind is so convinced of its idea when she prays, so completely accepts it, that contradiction or denial is impossible.

Of her many answered prayers during my lifetime, one stands out with great clarity, for it eliminated a serious and painful condition which had been before us for years.

As a child, my mother sustained an injury on a teeter- totter which resulted in a very troublesome and painful hernia that caused great discomfort and suffering during most of her waking hours. She consulted many doctors about her condition, but there was little in those days that could be done about a rupture.

This healing took place after an accident that occurred as we were building a new home.

My father and mother would to walk out each evening to see what progress was being made. On this particular evening, my mother neglected to put on her truss, which was very clumsy and difficult to wear.

The excavation for the basement had been completed and as she and my father stood near the edge looking into it, a piece of earth gave way under my mother's feet.

She lost her balance and fell into the hole.

My father rushed to her aid, but the hernia had come down and the pain was so great that she could not get up.

His first thought was to telephone for a cab to take her home, but there were no dwellings in the vicinity and the nearest drug store was eight blocks away. My mother realized that it would be a long wait and her problem of pain and immobility demanded immediate help.

"My God," said my father. "What shall we do?"

"Be still, John," she said. "God is here and He is going to take care of this for me."

Then she closed her eyes and prayed.

It seemed like an eternity to my father until she held up her hand and said, "Come, John, let us go home."

"Go home!" he said. "How can you walk over a mile in this condition?"

"Very easily," she replied.

"I have been healed. God has healed me."

My father was utterly dumfounded; he had seen her in such agony that he could not understand how she could be so calm and unaffected, or how she could possibly walk. They did walk home, however, and her hernia went up and never bothered her again.

That incident occurred fifty years ago, but I shall never forget the story as she told it to us children the next day. She said that as she prayed in the hole, the Christ Presence was so real and so near that she put her hand in His and was able to get up on her feet.

God is a very present help in time of trouble.

Ask, and it shall be given you; seek and ye shall find; knock, and it shall be opened unto you. For everyone that asketh receiveth; and he that seeketh findeth; and to "Him" that knocketh it shall be opened.

The command goes out to the whole world.

Like a great radio broadcast, it covers the earth, penetrating and interpenetrating everything and everybody.

But we often fail to realize that the command was given to each of us.

You ask. You seek. You knock.

In our eagerness to find help, we look to others. We want to discuss our problem with someone or we want someone else to help us meet it.

Then we get into a tight spot and stay there until we realize the Allness-of-God and find that nothing is lacking.

When we recognize "Him" as present in the place in which the trouble seems to be, He short-circuits it.

How often Jesus in His brief earthly ministry responded to the calls of the sick and healed them!

My little daughter lieth at the point of death: I pray thee, come and lay thy hands on her, that she may be healed; and she shall live.

The Centurion at Capernaum said:

"Speak the word only and my servant shall be healed".

A woman diseased with an issue of blood for twelve years touched the hem of His garment and was healed.

A leper said:

"Lord, if thou wilt, thou canst make me clean". Two blind men said:

"Thou son of David, have mercy on us".

A father said:

"Lord, have mercy on my son: for he is a lunatic, and sore vexed; for ofttimes he falleth into the fire, and oft into the water".

A woman of Canaan cried unto "Him", saying:

"Have mercy on me, O Lord, thou Son of David; my daughter is grievously vexed with a devil".

All these prayers were for healing and all were answered.

Teach us to pray:

In St. James 5:13, we are instructed to pray for ourselves:

Is any among you afflicted?

Let "Him" pray.

In St. James 5:16, we are told to pray for others:

Pray one for another, that ye may be healed.

In St. Mark 11:24, we are told to pray for anything and everything we want:

"What things soever ye desire, when ye pray, believe that ye receive them, and ye shall have them".

Do not the words, What things soever, include the healing of sickness and disease?

And what will you do with Jesus' promise in St. John 14:14, If ye shall ask anything in my name, I will do it"? The word anything would certainly include healing of the body and the Mind, wouldn't it?

But why did Jesus say:

"If ye shall ask anything in my name?"

Why in my name?

It was the night before His crucifixion that He first used these words in connection with a prayer or request and He used them six times.

It is obvious that He thought of this prayer as a prayer of tremendous and infinite possibilities.

It is significant too that this particular kind of prayer was something new. Hitherto, He said, have ye asked nothing in my name:

Ask, and ye shall receive, that your joy may be full.

In olden times the name of a person not only revealed the character of a person but his identity and his nature. To the Hebrews a name was thought to carry a certain power. Some names could be used to cast out demons and devils, and disease could be healed in the same way.

The words in my name mean literally to be in His Consciousness. Jesus said: "I and the Father are one." St. Paul said:

"It is no longer I that live but Christ liveth in me."

When we pray in His name, it is assumed that we are in His Presence, that we have that Mind in us which was also in "Him".

This power was brought out beautifully in the healing of the lame beggar at the gate of the temple. The beggar had asked for money and Peter said:

"Silver and gold have I none; but such as I have give I thee: In the name of Jesus Christ of Nazareth, rise up and walk."

Later he explained this healing by saying:

"His name through Faith in his name hath made this man strong, whom ye see and know: Yea, the Faith which is by "Him" hath given "Him" this perfect soundness in the presence of you all."

Weymouth translates the words in this way:

"By virtue of Faith in His name; His name has strengthened this man whom you behold and know: and the Faith which He has bestowed has entirely restored this man, as you can all see."

So name in this instance referred to the Christ in Peter's Consciousness who at his call healed the crippled beggar.

Such as I have give I thee speaks not only of Peter's Oneness with Christ but of his ability to impart that Consciousness to the crippled beggar. He had reached such a high state of Consciousness that he could act for Christ. He was so in tune with the Infinite that Christ operated through his word and the beggar was healed.

The effectual fervent prayer.

Do you see now why the effectual fervent prayer of a righteous man availeth much"? The effectual prayer is the prayer made in His name. It has the force and power to accomplish that whereunto it is sent. It does not mean wrestling or struggling with God; it means accepting "Him".

There is activity and life in the words; the very Presence of Christ enables them to realize that which they set out to do.

Do you believe it?

Then why relegate healing to doctors, to medicine and to hospitals?

Is God dead?

Has Christ lost his power?

Has the Holy Spirit abdicated?

Have the divine promises been abrogated? Read again II Chronicles 16: 12, 13.

"And Asa in the thirty and ninth year of his reign was diseased in his feet, until his disease was exceeding great: yet in his disease he sought not to the Lord, but to the physicians. And Asa slept with his fathers, and died in the one and fortieth year of his reign."

"That is ancient history," you say, but you are wrong. It is just as modern as today's newspaper.

Asa's sin was not that he had physicians but that he did not look first to the Lord.

His Faith was not in God but in man.

That does not mean that it was wrong for "Him" to have doctors and medicine but that he thought first about human help and material remedies.

He did not turn to God first; he did not see the Hand of God in the physicians on whom he called.

God Works on the Level of Our Understanding.

There are some schools of Spiritual therapy which are almost fanatical on the subject of calling a doctor.

They hold to the fallacious idea that to call a doctor shows a lack of Faith in God.

Why is this belief wrong?

Because Faith is the basic factor in all healing, and Faith works the way we use it.

It will work through a physician just as readily as it will work through a metaphysical practitioner; in either case, the means are secondary.

It is desirable, of course, to get healing through purely Spiritual means. But if you are unable to do this, if you have not arrived at the level of understanding that enables you to know your Oneness with the Source of health, if you are unable to meet the requirements of Spiritual Healing in a reasonable length of time, to refuse to call a doctor is like refusing to call the fire department to extinguish a fire.

In the first instance, you may get to Heaven ahead of time; in the second, you may lose your home.

Don't you see how inconsistent it is to allow yourself or someone near and dear to you to die because of Spiritual inadequacy when a mechanical adjustment, surgery or medical assistance, which are in themselves evidence of Divine Intelligence acting through man, could save a life?

I have seen such tragedies so many times that I feel justified in discussing the place of materia medica, and other healing agents.

I can't go along with the idea of refusing material aid, for the simple reason that there is nothing in the Bible to support it.

To eat figs for their laxative effect and thank God for them is an accepted practice, but to squeeze the juice out of figs, put it into a bottle and take it for the same purpose is construed as a sin by many persons.

The real issue is not whether we call a physician or don't call a physician, whether we take medicine or don't take medicine but whether we look first to the Lord, recognizing, as someone has said, "that all means combine to bring forth wholeness in the body and that each man must accommodate the means to his own understanding."

Think about that quotation for a moment and answer this question:

When you were sick, did you try God through prayer and Spiritual treatment first or did you turn at once to a doctor?

If you turned first to the doctor, did you recognize that God acted through "Him", and did you give God all the power and praise for the benefits you received?

Did you bless the medicine which the doctor prescribed for you and see it as a means of stimulating your Faith?

Jesus used mud which He made from the spittle of His mouth to heal the blind man.

He used a fishing pole, a fish and Peter to get the tax money.

He used five loaves and two fishes to feed five thousand hungry people.

Elisha told Naaman to dip in the Jordan river seven times.

Isn't it possible for God to use material means in the healing of one who is not yet able to put his entire dependence upon Spirit?

Medicine, doctors and metaphysical practitioners are just different means to help us become conscious of the Power that transcends and heals sickness and disease.

All healing in the final analysis is Spiritual healing.

We do not know why some people are healed through Spiritual means and others are not any more than doctors know why some people are healed through one form of medical treatment and others fail to receive help.

But in none of these failures can we blame God or believe in the failure of His Power, The failure is always within the person seeking healing. He does not meet the requirements of healing; he has not cooperated sufficiently with the Grace of God.

Since the Law is eternally in operation, there is no reason why we should not be healed by Faith if our desires, motives and belief are of the right kind.

We must make sure that we are seeking God for "Him"self and not for the loaves and fishes.

We must make sure that we have made the right adjustment to Life.

We must make sure that our vision is single to Truth and that we realize body, soul and Spirit as a Divine Unity.

We must make sure that our Faith is strong enough to enable us to depend entirely upon God.

Are you troubled by the question as to whether you should or should not call a doctor?

Then settle it this way:

If you are still in the material (human) Consciousness and feel the need of a doctor, by all means call one.

If you were wholly in Spiritual (Christ) Consciousness, you would not ask the question.

Material Consciousness and Spiritual Consciousness are not two different kinds of Consciousness but are varying degrees of the same Consciousness.

We cannot expect the full blessing of God until we are wholly in His Consciousness.

While we are raising the level of our Consciousness, there is no reason why we cannot accept our good in any form.

There is no reason why, if necessity demands it, we cannot cooperate with a doctor of medicine just as effectively as we do with a doctor of the soul, or with both at the same time.

One of the weaknesses of metaphysical students is the tendency to go beyond their mental equivalents, to imagine that they have arrived at a state of Spiritual Consciousness which as yet they have only glimpsed. What does the Bible say to such people?

It says, Lean not unto thine own [human] understanding.

I quote a prominent physician who is himself a deep student of metaphysics:

"I believe absolutely in metaphysical science up to the point of the patient's understanding, but I have no patience whatever with those who try to go beyond it, with those who wait for healing until all hope has gone."

In other words, we must keep our Spiritual feet on the ground.

Until our knowledge of Truth is absolute and our Faith is one-pointed, we should use all the means of healing at our command and thank God for them.

The functions of medicine and metaphysics are identical. Both assist Nature and provide the conditions through which God can heal.

All means of healing produce only what we expect them to produce.

They are stimulants to our Faith.

When we have in us the Mind which was also in Christ Jesus, when our Consciousness no longer takes account of sickness, we shall no longer need medicine or metaphysics.

"But," someone asks:

"How can we put God first when we call a doctor and take medicine?"

We can see both the doctor and medicine as channels for the operation of the healing power of God.

We can know that we are never at any time dependent upon the means but are always dependent upon the Life, Love, Law, Truth and Power of God, who forgiveth all our iniquities, who healeth all our diseases.

Dean Claude Flaherty says that:

"All diseases are ultimately curable, and that in the meantime failure to heal is due to a fault in the instruments or channels, not to the Agent and Source of healing, which is Christ."

Another question which is often asked is why people get sick.

We have the answer in the Scriptures:

For this cause many are weak and sickly among you, and many sleep . . . not discerning the body of Christ.

It is wonderful to know that when we stop looking to the body of John Smith and look to the body of Christ, we shall be healed.

To whom was the command, Physician, heal thyself, addressed?

It was addressed to the single-eyed, those who are one with God, those who realize the Divine Unity of body, soul and Spirit. If thine eye be single [one- pointed to Truth] thy whole body shall be full of light.

When St. Paul said:

"There is a natural [material] body and there is a Spiritual body [Christ Body]", he was not talking about two different bodies—one in Heaven and one on earth—but of two states of Consciousness.

Those in the natural or material Consciousness think of themselves as having two bodies—one here and one somewhere else. Those in the Spiritual Consciousness think of the natural (material) body as the Spiritual Body unrealized.

To them, Jesus gave the command:

"Physician, heal thyself."

St. Paul said:

"To be absent from the [material] body is to be present with the Lord [Christ Body] and Christ in you, the hope of glory."

When the Mind is single to the Body of Christ, the saying, It is no longer I that live but Christ liveth in me, is fulfilled.

Perception of the Christ Body is the metamorphosis of the sick body to a body of health and wholeness.

The Christ Body is not the product of human imagination or thought but the Word made flesh.

It is easier for some people to believe in the tangible than in the intangible, to have more Faith in man than in God, to have more confidence in medicine than in Mind.

A pill acts more quickly for them than a metaphysical treatment.

They are still in the material or human Consciousness; the concrete is more real to them than the abstract.

What has brought this state about? The habit of belief.

What shall they do about it? They can do three things:

First: They must not go beyond their mental equivalents. They must be content to demonstrate on the level of their understanding.

Second: They must change their habit of belief. They must start thinking of themselves as they are in Spirit and cultivate a greater confidence in Christ.

Third: They must be sensible and use material means as long as they are needed. When these materially Minded persons develop more Faith in the power of Spirit than in the power of matter, they will discard material means unconsciously.

Do you see now why Asa slept with his fathers?

It was not because he called the doctors but because he did not give the power to God.

The Law states very plainly, Power [all power] belongeth unto God.

The Lord our God is one Lord.

He is a jealous God in the sense that he will not share his Power with another.

Why?

Because anything we ascribe power to becomes another God.

The Lord he is God: there is none else. There can't be God and something else.

If there were two powers instead of one, the Universe would fall apart.

It doesn't make any difference whether you call a metaphysician, medic, osteopath, chiropractor or surgeon, healing is Spiritual.

It is God's power acting through the means, together with the power of your Faith, that does the work.

Metaphysics, medicine, osteopathy and surgery are just different modes of expressions of the One Power; all lead back to It.

The doctor of medicine refers to this Power as vis medicatrix naturae.

The metaphysician calls It "the Divine impulse toward wholeness." St. Paul called It Christ in you.

Prove me now herewith.

Would you know the Christ Body?

Then feel after "Him" until you find "Him".

The moment you touch "Him" in your Consciousness, He touches you.

Christ is the medium through which God works. He is the Saviour, Counsellor, and Revelator.

He is the great leavening, resurrecting, purifying and transforming power of God.

When you entertain Christ in Consciousness, you have a magnetic compulsion.

You attract to yourself the factors that will help you to accomplish whatever you set out to do.

To embody the Christ is to share the fruitage of Christ.

To know "Him" as the Reality of your own Consciousness is to overcome the world. Have you found the Christ?

No?

Then keep up the search until you find "Him". When He is perceived and realized.

He becomes the Son of God appearing AS YOU.

How shall you know when you are entertaining the Christ in Consciousness?

Ask yourself these questions:

Am I easier to get along with than I was?

Has my disposition improved?

Have I lost the capacity for anger, meanness, animosity, faultfinding, bitterness, criticism, jealousy, ill-will and enmity?

Is my health better?

Do I have greater supply?

Do I work with less personal effort?

Do people like me better?

If you have the Christ, you have results, for acceptance of Christ and results always go hand in hand.

What is the secret of being touched by Christ?

You have the answer in St. Paul's words, It is no longer I that live but Christ liveth in me.

What is this I that has suddenly stopped living?

It is the human self which Jesus said must be denied and which St. Paul said must be put off.

Only as you develop Spiritual awareness can you be touched by Christ in Consciousness.

Only then can the Father reach out and change the circumstance world through you.

Only then can Christ appear AS YOU.

There are certain fields beyond which medical science has not gone.

"I can cure some things," says the medical practitioner, "but when you come to the incurable diseases, ray power is still limited."

Well, where do we go from here? Is this the end of the road?

Is there no other source to which we can turn?

What will we say to the desolate and helpless persons who have come to the end of medical resources?

We will tell them about the healing power of Faith and the Spiritual therapy of Truth.

We will tell them about the thousands of "incurables" who have been cured by Spiritual means.

We will tell them about the many persons who have outlived the doctors who had given them up.

We will quote such renowned medical men as Alexis Carrel who in Reflections on Life said:

"Prayer acts not only on our affective states but also on the physiological processes. Sometimes it cures organic diseases in a few instants or a few days. However incomprehensible these phenomena may be, we are forced to admit their reality.

The Bureau of Medical Testimony at Lourdes has registered more than two hundred cases of tuberculosis, blindness or osteomyelitis, cancer and other organic diseases whose almost instantaneous cure is undisputed.

Here we are on solid ground. Man needs help: he prays; the help comes. Whatever its future interpretation may be, this fact remains eternally true."

We will show them how man's extremity is God's opportunity and how He takes hold when man lets go.

We will prove through the Scriptures that bodily healing is just as much a part of the Divine plan as Spiritual development.

We will prove to them that the prayer of Faith shall save the sick, and that all things are possible to "Him" that believeth.

What Faith Does:

One of the things we discover in reading the Bible is that Faith is the first requirement for doing or accomplishing anything.

Without Faith, we cannot be healed. Without Faith, we cannot be prospered. Without Faith we cannot pray effectively. Without Faith we cannot live triumphantly. Without Faith we cannot know God. Without Faith, we cannot please "Him".

Without Faith we cannot claim His promises. Without Faith, we cannot be "saved".

By Faith Abel offered . . .

By Faith Enoch was translated.

By Faith Noah . . . prepared an ark. By Faith Abraham . . . went out.

By Faith he sojourned . . .

By Faith Abraham, when he was tried, offered up Isaac.

By Faith Isaac blessed Jacob and Esau concerning things to come.

By Faith Jacob, when he was dying, blessed both the sons of Joseph.

By Faith Moses . . . was hid three months of his parents.

By Faith we attract whatever we identify ourselves with.

By Faith God answers us in terms of our belief about life.

By Faith we make or remake our lives.

By Faith we choose health or sickness.

By Faith we choose prosperity or poverty.

By Faith we choose success or failure.

By Faith we advance or retreat.

In its static form, Faith is neutral and impersonal. Anyone can use Faith for any purpose.

Faith has no choice or desire of its own.

Faith will remain static (inactive) until it is put to work, and it cares not by whom or for what it is used.

Faith becomes active when one meets the conditions and sets it in motion.

But the requirements of Faith must be met.

There must be absolute conformity to Faith Principle.

Faith will move in any direction Mind gives it. Faith will accomplish anything Mind decrees. Faith will do anything that Mind directs.

When Faith is directed toward God, man gains access to unlimited power.

Working with Principle, Faith knows how to build a successful business.

Faith knows how to turn ideas into cash.

Faith knows how to take a sick body and make it well.

Faith knows how to take a failure and turn it into a success.

Faith does not have to argue or reason.

Faith knows and knows that it knows.

There is no limit to the power of the Principle of Faith.

Faith will take a man to where he wants to be or leave "Him" where he is.

The only limiting factor is unbelief.

When man realizes that All-of-God is wherever he is and that he is indwell by this Allness, disease and all other forms of evil lose their power over "Him".

He experiences a sense of security and well-being he has never before imagined.

When he glimpses the vastness of the Power within "Him", nothing is impossible to "Him".

When he realizes that the same Power that holds the stars in their courses can free his body from sickness, he knows, as someone has said:

"There are no incurable diseases—only incurable people, incurable because they remain blind to their potential healing."

Why do we say that Faith is the first requirement in demonstrating Truth?

We have the answer in Hebrews 11:6:

"Without Faith it is impossible to please "Him": for he that cometh to God [enters into Oneness with "Him"] must believe [have Faith] that he is, and that he is a rewarder of them that diligently seek "Him".

To come to God (to enter his Consciousness), we must first believe that there is a God and that He hears and answers our prayers.

To have Faith in God means to have a constant dependence and reliance upon "Him", to have absolute belief in His word and unqualified acceptance of His promises.

Do you recall that Jesus rebuked the disciples for their lack of Faith?

In St. Mark 4:40, we read that He asked them:

"Why are ye so fearful? How is it that ye have no Faith?"

In St. Luke 8:25, we hear "Him" demand:

"Where is your Faith?"

After He had calmed the storm that terrified them. St. Luke 18:8 records a sad and searching question.

After telling them a parable to this end that men ought always to pray and not to faint and promising that God would avenge those who cry day and night unto "Him", He asked:

"When the Son of man cometh, shall he find Faith on the earth?"

St. Mark 16:14 tells us that Jesus upbraided them with their unbelief and hardness of heart because they believed not them which had seen "Him" after he was risen.

Did you ever make the mistake of trying to compare your Faith with the Faith of another?

Did you ever say, "I wish I had the Faith that so-and- so has"?

Then stop making comparisons.

Know that your Faith is the same Faith that everybody else has.

Your Faith is the same Faith that Jesus had.

His Faith was more highly developed than yours, but it is precisely the same Faith.

Yes, the same Faith that Jesus used to do His mighty works is your Faith now.

Does that thought startle you? Then verify it for yourself.

The Bible tells us that God is no respecter of persons. They were all filled with the Holy Ghost at Pentecost.

The manifestation of the Spirit is given to every man to profit withal. St. Paul told the Corinthians that God's promise is to you and to your children.

When God makes a promise, He keeps it. His guarantees are always fulfilled.

When you are told that you can have anything you ask in Faith, why don't you prove it?

Why do you tarry?

Why don't you get your desires and your prayers in accord?

Why don't you stand boldly on the promise until He answers?

Is it because you still feel that your belief is inadequate and imperfect?

Then dismiss such a thought from your Mind.

Read St. Mark 9:24-27 carefully and you will see that it is possible to have belief and unbelief at the same time and still get results.

Remember the father, seeking healing for his dumb son, who said, Lord, I believe, help thou mine unbelief?

His prayer was answered.

The promise, If ye have Faith as a grain of mustard seed . . . nothing shall be impossible unto you, leaves plenty of room for both doubt and belief.

In fact, you can have a little of both and still get results. Don't you see what Jesus is saying here?

He is telling us that God answers our prayers not in proportion to our unbelief but in proportion to our Faith.

Emerson says:

"There is no great and no small To the Soul that maketh all."

However, our Faith naturally expands and grows stronger as we put it into use and see its power.

It feeds on our acceptance, persistency and trust.

A strongly held desire, persisted in and backed up by whatever Faith you have is as certain of fulfilment as that day follows night.

But remember, He that wavereth is like the wave of the sea, driven by the wind and tossed: let not that man think that he shall receive anything of the Lord.

I should like to share with you here a true story of a young couple who proved the power of the Law of Faith.

They married with the desire to have a family but the almost immediate death of the father in both their homes threw a financial responsibility upon them which made them feel it necessary to delay establishing a home of their own.

When this was lightened and they were able to move into the home which they had bought and paid for before their marriage, they were told by physicians that it was physically impossible for them to have a child. Nothing doubting, they bought a baby chest and each pay day before they faced the family budget shopped together for something that a new baby might need.

Of course, their desire was granted.

What door could withstand that persistent knocking—the knocking of prayer and of the overt evidence of Faith in that prayer?

By the time the baby was born, the chest was more than filled with beautiful and carefully selected evidences of their Faith.

He was a true Faith baby coming into the world easily and soon showing an unusually high intelligence.

The family prospered financially and without undue effort on their part the boy was graduated from one of our most select engineering schools with top honours.

A MEASURING ROD FOR FAITH

Please take your pencil and grade yourself honestly on each question in one of these ways: 1. Yes. 2. To some degree. 3. No. Work on the area in which you fall short until you can give an affirmative answer.

Do I believe that the Law of Faith acts upon my word?

Do I have a deep conviction that GOD'S GOOD IS IN INSTANT MANIFESTATION?

Do I believe that I have the right to have what I ask? Do I have great expectations?

Do I know that what I believe will be demonstrated? Do I trust the Law of Life to supply my needs?

Do I believe in the authority of my word and my right to command the power of God which acts subjectively for me?

Do I believe that the answer to all my problems is within myself?

Do I have a deep conviction that all that the Father hath is mine?

Do I believe that Life answers me in terms of my belief about it?

Do I leave the delivery of my good to God? Do I place all my dependence upon "Him"?

Do I empty my Mind of all contrary and negative thoughts so that the Law of Faith can operate without interference?

Do I strive to prove the power of my Faith through every thought, action and feeling?

Do I stand unmoved in a condition until I am master of it?

Do I believe that I have dominion? Do I believe in my right to succeed?

Do I have a definite purpose in prayer? Do I expect fulfillment now?

Are all the forces of my being moving with my desire?

When you can answer these questions in the affirmative, you will win no matter what the odds, for: GOD WORKS THROUGH FAITH.

The need for physical healing probably initiates the search for God more often than any other one cause.

But healing is not an end in itself.

Healing is a by-product of accepting and realizing the Wholeness of the Perfect Man.

It makes no difference what motivates the search.

One personal experience in applying the Law of Faith encourages that questing, searching, demanding Spirit which we house to the point that it is never satisfied until it has found itself in the greater Spirit, until it has given Truth a home, until it is expressed in the abundant life.

What Do You Know!

Through Faith, you learn:

1. That the greatest commandment in the Decalogue is Thou shalt have no other gods before me.

2. That the greatest Power in the universe is the Unconditioned Power of God.

3. That the greatest activity is the activity of Truth.

4. That the greatest action is the action of Inaction.

5. That the greatest stabilizer in man's life is the knowledge of the Unchanging God, of God as Law.

6. That the greatest creative factor man possesses is his ability to conceive in thought and to become that which he has conceived.

7. That the greatest force in his life is his Consciousness of Oneness with God.

In The Impatient Dawn, Walter C. Lanyon says:

"The complete submission to the ways of God leads to the Perfect Way and brings out the true meaning of I am the way. It is only at this elevation that the laws which Jesus gave can be and are made manifest as realities. It is then that whatsoever you designate the I AM to be, you are. The urge of this designation is coming through, straight from the God of the Universe, guiding you into the things that have been prepared for you and which have never entered into the heart of man."

From Belief to Realization:

When we accept the promises of God literally and personally through our Faith, when we associate ourselves with Jesus Christ to whom God was as real as was His mother, when we let the Mind be in us which was also in "Him", we develop the Consciousness of the Presence of God.

We find in Christ the perpetual Incarnation, the revelation of an unseen but Eternal Presence. Hear ye "Him" was the command of God.

As we accept Jesus' statement:

118

"I and the Father are one".

We pass from belief in God to the realization of God. In this process, we have accepted our belief as Reality, have completed it in our Consciousness, and have felt it so deeply that it was planted in the subjective Mind and took form in one experience.

The poet Wordsworth beautifully described the man who has arrived at this state as:

"One in whom persuasion and belief had ripened into Faith; and Faith become a passionate intuition."

Realization starts in the conscious Mind and becomes full-orbed in the Subconscious Mind.

In the realization of God, there is no room for thought of poverty, sickness, lack or limitation.

There is room only for the things of God. Do you remember Jesus' prayer:

"Father, glorify thou me with thine own self with the glory which I had with thee before the world was?"

One who expresses the glory of God's Allness truly lives, moves and has his being in "Him".

We have the choice between the endless round of overcoming something or dwelling in the Consciousness in which there is nothing to overcome. Can you imagine anything lacking in the Allnessof- God?

The primary purpose of Spiritual therapy is to establish the Consciousness of Oneness with this Allness. The goal of every student of Truth is to comprehend, accept and express the Allness-of-God.

As we approach the goal, we begin to understand the meaning of Jesus' words, Son, thou art ever with me and all that I have is thine.

119

By Faith we come to see that God is not apart from us but together with us.

We come to see that He is not only near but here. We, pass from immanence to Presence.

When the Presence is realized, the boundaries of matter disappear.

No longer accepting the appearance for the fact, and no longer depending upon visible things for support, we recognize matter as the obedient servant of our word and receive abundantly from Spirit.

God will always be to us what we conceive "Him" to be. He acts only upon the level of Consciousness which we provide.

The higher our level, the greater His power in us.

When our concept of God includes Life, Love, Truth, Knowledge, Understanding, Law and Principle, it is so absolute that it transcends all limitations.

God is "His" own affirmation. God only knows: I AM.

He doesn't know anything else, for there is nothing else to know.

When you pray in the Consciousness that I and the Father are one, your prayer is already answered. When you are so convinced of your prayer that you believe it yourself, all things are yours.

When your prayer touches the Consciousness of Reality, it is instantly fulfilled.

When the God that is within you at this instant rules absolutely in your life, you partake of the Divine Substance.

Some teachers use the terms realization and Consciousness interchangeably but there is an important difference between them. Realization is the integrating factor of the Mind.

It is that which gives the soul of the idea roots. Consciousness, on the other hand, is the awareness and embodiment of that which has been realized.

The purpose of both realization and Consciousness is to express God in the outer world.

"In that day ye shall know that I am in the Father, and ye in me and I in you".

In this vision of totality, we realize that all power is given to the Son.

In this Three-in-One Consciousness, we are able to do the greater things which were promised in His Name.

We have an abiding sense of the Presence and know true companionship with God.

When we detach ourselves sufficiently from our physical existence, we quickly recover our Consciousness of Oneness.

We are emancipated from our human limitations.

We realize that GOD IS EVERYWHERE EQUALLY PRESENT, and look to "Him" as the Only Power.

Most of us accept God in our heads, but that is only half the process. The other half is to accept "Him" as the centre of our being.

When we put self in the centre, we draw disease and misfortune as a magnet draws steel filings the self falls apart.

When we get the centre right, everything else falls into its right place.

When we make the contact with God, we identify ourselves with "Him".

In this Unity, we learn to say "My God," not "Oh, God."

With the first expression, we know the solution existed before the problem appeared; with the second, we face the problem only.

Who is content to live in a world that gets smaller and smaller?

Who would not prefer to live in an enlarging world— a world in which everything good multiplies in his hands, a world in which Love of God motivates his every action, a world in which he stops working for Love of self and does everything for the Love of God?

And now abideth Faith, hope, charity; these three; but the greatest of these is charity.

You may wonder that charity is counted as greater than Faith if you think of it as the word is commonly used today, but listen to the definition for the word charity given by Webster's New International Dictionary:

"The virtue or act of loving God with a Love which transcends that for creatures, and of loving others for the sake of God. Act of loving, or disposition to Love all men as brothers because they are sons of God; Love of fellow men."

The word charity comes from the Latin "caritas" which means Love and is all embracing, as you see.

Do you remember St. Paul's words, Faith that worketh by Love?

Through your Faith, you give Truth a home; you organize ideas and apply principles.

Personal experience is always the pragmatic test of Faith.

God is Life but Life must be expressed.

God is Love, but Love must manifest Itself. Emerson said:

"What we commonly call man, the eating, drinking, planting, counting man, does not, as we know him, represent himself, but misrepresents himself."

Faith convinces you that He who made man in his image and likeness did not intend for you to represent disease, misery and death but to demonstrate health, peace, and life.

Jesus said:

"I am come that ye might have life and have it more abundantly."

That is good news. It means that:

YOU DO NOT HAVE TO STAY THE WAY YOU ARE.

The whole New Testament is an affirmation of that Truth.

In the first four Books, the disciples tell others of the wonderful things that have happened to them. They say, "In Him, we speak with new tongues, we become a new creature, old things are passed away and all things are become new."

The Truth that the New Testament presents is the power to change anything that needs to be changed, to adjust anything that needs to be adjusted, to heal anything that needs to be healed, to save anything that needs to be saved.

That is good news indeed, isn't it?

It is good news for everyone, no matter what he wishes to change in his life.

It is good news for the diseased, for the alcoholic, for the maladjusted, for the handicapped, for the misfit, for the hard-pressed, for the mediocre, for the discouraged, for the unloved, for the down-trodden.

YOU DO NOT NEED TO STAY THE WAY YOU ARE.

I am thinking right now about you who are reading this book.

I am thinking about those of you who may be discouraged, frightened, demoralized, defeated, bewildered, broken-hearted, of all those who still wonder if there is any hope, if there is any use in trying since the problem is so big and the Faith so small.

Oh, my friends, put yourselves in the way of being found by God. Let "Him" get into and under your lives.

He will make a whole new world for you.

Can you think of anything more thrilling than that people like you and me can rise above our difficulties and triumph over our troubles?

Well, give yourself another chance on a higher level. The delay in achieving victory is not God's but yours. What is it that is worrying you right now as you read this book? It doesn't make any difference what it is.

YOU DO NOT NEED TO STAY THE WAY YOU ARE.

Heaven is not attained by having glands corrected, complexes straightened out or allergies cured, but by letting this Mind be in you which was also in Christ Jesus.

When materia medica fails man, the Faith in a Power greater than himself, inherent in him, causes him to turn to Immateria Medicato that which lies beyond the material, to the healing that comes directly from God by impartation.

Through your Faith and realization, you know that you do not have to go to Church to find God, nor do you have to get someone else to treat you.

You have the understanding, the belief and acceptance.

You know that you have only to release the God in you so that He can manifest AS YOU. You take Jesus' command, Leave all and follow me, literally.

You think of God very simply and very directly as the Power by which you live, move, and have your being; you recognize "Him" as the Inner Principle of your life and know that He is spontaneously responsive to your every need.

When you stop lying about yourself, there is nothing left but Truth, and that is God. When you stop believing in sickness, there is nothing left but Health; that is God.

When you stop being fearful, there is nothing left but Faith; that is God.

When you stop worrying, there is nothing left but Peace; that is God.

In such degree as your Oneness with "Him" is realized, it automatically demonstrates Itself.

Back of every appearance is the fact, or God. Back of this body is a Spiritual body.

Back of these ears are Spiritual ears. Back of these eyes are Spiritual eyes.

Faith tells you that when you think and live in the Consciousness of Spirit, the perfection of Spirit will appear in your body, for it is there all the time awaiting your demand upon it.

In this Consciousness, you know that while disease is a fact in your experience, it is not the Truth and that you are bound to it only by your thought.

You know that you do not get something for nothing, and that without a true mental equivalent of what you want you cannot have it. Signs follow them that believe. The signs that appear in your experience are in line with your belief.

You realize that everything is in Divine Order and you plant this knowledge in your Subconscious Mind; you know too that you must be consistent and persistent in your realization.

125

The Apostle says:

"If any of you lack wisdom, let him ask of God who giveth to all men liberally and upbraideth not; and it shall be given him. But let him ask in Faith, nothing wavering. For he that wavereth is like a wave of the sea driven with the wind and tossed. For let that man not think that he shall receive anything of the Lord."

You know you must persist until your Subconscious Mind has accepted the desire as fulfilled, for the Universe will be measured out to you with your own measure.

"With what measure ye mete, it shall be measured to you again . . . As thou hast believed, so be it done unto you."

If Jesus hadn't known that the man with the palsy could get up and walk, he couldn't have walked even when Jesus commanded him to walk. The power was not in the command, Arise, but in the belief or mental equivalent that Jesus held.

In Faith, you know that the Presence doesn't know anything about big and little. It simply knows Itself.

You know that you attract to yourself what you are. Having found Faith, you do not complain when the answer to a specific prayer is delayed.

You examine the foundation upon which your Faith rests, knowing that Faith which is active and alive always works. You analyze the situation in your own thought to see what is blocking your answer. You ask and honestly answer these questions:

Can a child of God made in His image and likeness be lacking in Faith?

Do I know the Truth and know that I know?

Do I have fixity of vision and invincibility of purpose? Do I have persistency?

Do I believe that God wants to help me?

Do I believe that He has power to help me? Do I believe that He will help me?

Have I removed all doubt, fear, negation and depression from my Mind?

Is my Faith one-pointed?

Do I believe in One Power?

Do I reject the contrary evidence of the senses? Do I accept my Oneness with God?

Do I trust "Him" sufficiently to leave everything in His care?

Do I thank "Him" every day for the Faith and understanding I already have and the capacity to grow in Faith and understanding?

When you find what is lacking, you supply it. When you find what is wrong, you remedy it.

But you do not challenge the power of Faith nor your own worthiness to receive what you ask for.

You follow the injunction, Stir up the gift of God which is in thee, knowing that God hath not given us the Spirit of fear; but of power and of Love, and of a sound Mind.

You stir up your gift of Faith.

You rouse it into action by praise and thanksgiving. You act on your Faith for your highest good and for the good of others.

You put Faith to work in little as well as big problems in your everyday affairs.

You learn to live by indirection. Consider the lilies.

Do you know what it means to live by indirection?

Do you know what it means to work by not working? Consider the lilies of the field how they grow.

They grow not by striving or straining, but by being what they already are.

"They toil not neither do they spin yet I say unto you that even Solomon in all his glory was not arrayed like one of these. The lily seeks one thing— to be all that a lily can be."

Jesus didn't say to consider the beauty or the perfume of the lilies but to consider how they grow.

Well, how do they grow?

They toil not, neither do they spin, They grow by labourless activity; they grow without effort and without strain.

Jesus asked you to consider the lilies to emphasize the importance of letting Life live in you AS YOU.

The commands are Stand still and see the salvation of the Lord and Be still and know.

Most prayer tends to be a matter of personal will and effort— begging, beseeching, petitioning.

Jesus said:

"Seek ye first the kingdom of God" [the awareness of the Finished Kingdom].

Start there.

When you get the Centre right and move outward from It, when you realize that what you are seeking is already yours, you live by indirection.

You do not have to labour and struggle to bring your good into visibility. You have only to remove the obstructions in its path.

The Divine Power you are calling on is effortless; human effort only slows it down.

Emerson said:

"A little consideration of what takes place around us every day would show us that our painful labours are unnecessary and fruitless; that only in our easy, simple, spontaneous action are we strong, and that by contenting ourselves with obedience we become divine. Belief and Love, a believing Love will relieve us of a vast load of care. 0 my brothers, God exists.

Place yourself in the middle of the stream of power and wisdom which animates all whom it floats, and you are without effort impelled to truth, to right and a perfect contentment." . . . "It is only the finite that has wrought and suffered; the Infinite lies in smiling repose."

I change not.

In this rapidly changing, bewildering world, our Faith finds reassurance in such words as these:

Heaven and earth shall pass away but my words shall not pass away.

I am the Lord; I change not. The Lord shall endure forever.

I will never leave thee nor forsake thee. Lo, I am with you always.

His truth endureth to all generations.

His mercy endureth forever.

The goodness of God endureth continually.

The eternal God is thy refuge and thy strength.

Before the mountains were brought forth or ever thou hadst formed the earth and the world, even from everlasting to everlasting, thou art God.

Before Abraham was, I am.

I am God, and there is none else.

I am Alpha and Omega, the beginning and the ending, saith the Lord, which is, and which was, and which is to come, the Almighty.

Circumstances change, environment changes, the weather and the climate change; and we change with the times, adjusting to the new, adapting our way of living to the situation, accommodating ourselves to new modes of travel, to new foods and new methods of preparing old foods, to new services in our homes, and responding to new ideas.

Flexibility is a quality with which we were endowed at birth. But God does not change.

It is true that man's concept of God changed materially with the coming of Jesus and that it is still growing and expanding. It will continue to do so for us today as long as our Consciousness grows and expands and our ability to perceive and receive more and more of His Power increases.

Man's idea of God has always kept pace with his own development.

The God of the ancients was a tribal God; today we accept literally the words: "The Lord our God is one Lord", and have developed ideals of the One World, of the Brotherhood of Man, of respect for individual dignity and worth.

Signs follow these emerging concepts in the form of such activities as Food Lifts, Red Cross, Aid to Dependent Children, Social Security, and Old Age Pensions.

The freedom that Jesus promised us as we learned the Truth is nowhere more evident or more significant than in the departure from the concept of the jealous God of the Old Testament who visited the iniquities of the fathers upon the children unto the third and fourth generation.

The guilt complex, the belief in original sin and in predestination have embittered and shattered countless lives. The far-off God pictured on our Sunday School cards as an old man with a long beard has become the Father Within who upbraideth not.

We have learned to see that our mistakes result from our stage of development at the time we make them and realize that punishment is merely consequence. We face the mistake and do what we can to correct it.

We do not indulge in an orgy of self-condemnation, hug the mistake close to us for years, or use it as an alibi for weakness the rest of our lives.

We learn from it; we resolve to go up higher . . . to go and sin no more.

We act then on the new level of Consciousness which we have attained.

Faith in the Father Within and in our Oneness with "Him" enables us to see ourselves as a new creature.

Accepting through Faith our place in the order of creation as instruments through which God takes form upon the earth gives our lives purpose, dignity, meaning.

At the same time it adds the responsibility of making good use of the Power and of being a worthy instrument.

For while we were created in his Spiritual image and likeness, we were given the power of choice, will power, the ability of self-determination.

Because we have Faith, we choose wisely to rise above the material and physical self, which is of the earth earthy, and to accept the dominion given to us at creation.

In no area of daily living is evidence of our Faith more demanded than in our relationships with others.

If we are exercising our Faith, we do not immediately think of the possibility of an accident when a Loved one is late, of the need to get a contract in writing lest we be cheated; we do not nod our heads and exude sympathy as a friend elaborates on his sad physical state and enumerates his symptoms. We do not shy away from a stranger because we do not like his looks. We do not condemn or judge the action of another.

We know that GOD IS EVERYWHERE EQUALLY PRESENT and surrender the Loved one to his care.

If our imaginations must work, we put them to work on the Good that might have caused the delay—the meeting an old and Loved friend, the opportunity to serve, a promising business deal.

We accord to another the same Perfection that we accept for ourselves and meet sick friend and stranger with the quick reminder:

"Perfect God—Perfect Being; Perfect Man, never sick, never dying."

We know that Right Action is God's Action and that those of us who are working together in a business deal all move in the One Mind to express Right Action.

We greet the unprepossessing stranger with the thought, "The God in me salutes the God in you."

Our Faith tells us that as surely as there is a phase of man that faces the outer world (the five senses), there is another phase which faces God through which we can enter into union with "Him".

132

Through Faith we have constant realization of the Presence of God.

This is Eternal life, that they might know thee, the only true God and Jesus Christ whom Thou hast sent.

That I might know "Him" was St. Paul's greatest ambition.

We know is the triumphant ring of every paragraph in St. John's first epistle.

Through our Faith, we are able to say with the disciples, we have found the Messiahs, which is . . . Christ.

CPSIA information can be obtained
at www.ICGtesting.com
Printed in the USA
BVHW081139170920
588935BV00005B/558